# Low-Carb
# Vegetarian

*Margo DeMello*

Book Publishing Company
Summertown, Tennessee

Book Publishing Company
P.O. Box 99
Summertown, TN 38483
1-888-260-8458

Printed in Canada

ISBN 1-57067-167-2
09   08   07   06   05   04                    6   5   4   3   2   1

Library of Congress Cataloging-in-Publication Data
DeMello, Margo.
  Low-carb vegetarian / by Margo DeMello.
       p. cm.
  Includes bibliographical references and index.
  ISBN 1-57067-167-2
  1. Vegetarian cookery. 2. Low-carbohydrate diet--Recipes. I. Title.

  TX837.D36 2004
  641.5'636--dc22                              2004012139

# Table of Contents

Thanks to

My husband, Tom Young, for supporting me in every way;

My parents, Bill DeMello and Robin Montgomery; my sister, Vicki DeMello; and my sister-in-law, Merah Chung, for sending me recipes;

Kate Turlington and her colleagues at PETA for testing my recipes;

Anita Carswell, Carla Brauer, Erin Williams, Andy Page and Karen Courtemanche for testing my food;

Martin Rowe at Lantern for recommending my publisher;

Bob and Cynthia Holzapfel for taking a chance on me.

# Why a Low-Carb Vegetarian Cookbook?

Americans are obsessed with weight—and for good reason. Americans are among the fattest individuals in the industrialized world, with more than 130 million overweight or obese adults in 2001, along with 8.8 million overweight children. According to the Centers for Disease Control and Prevention, up to 64% of all adult Americans are overweight and 30% of children are also overweight. The diet and nutrition industry is likewise enormous, bringing in profits of over forty million dollars per year, with an expected growth rate of 5.8% per year.

Today, the biggest trend in the diet industry and among dieters is an emphasis on eating a limited amount of carbohydrates, popularized by the Atkins diet, the South Beach diet, Carbohydrate Addicts, and the Zone. All of these espouse, to greater or lesser degrees, reducing or eliminating many carbohydrates from the diet, particularly starchy, grain-based carbohydrates. While the Atkins diet in particular is very controversial due to its reliance on high-fat, animal-based proteins such as meat, butter, and cheese, and its almost religious avoidance of almost all carbohydrates, numerous studies have shown that curbing carbohydrates (and especially highly processed carbohydrates) can be an effective weight loss method, and, when done correctly, can promote a healthful way of eating.

Low-carb cookbooks are one of the largest growing adjuncts of this industry, with hundreds of cookbooks geared to both devotees of the popular low-carb diets[1] as well as to customers who simply want to cut down on their carbohydrate intake. Yet not a single one of these cookbooks is geared to vegetarians or to those who are trying to eat less meat.

---

1 It is estimated that approximately 24 million Americans are now on some kind of low–carb diet program, according to a 2003 survey by Opinion Dynamics Corporation.

Many vegetarians, just like meat eaters, are plagued with weight problems. And many vegetarians eat an unhealthful diet based on white flour, sugar, fried foods, and fast food snacks. Just like meat eaters, these vegetarians need to be more nutrition conscious, and many find that the typical low-fat vegetarian cookbook is too rigid or doesn't work for them.

If you're like me—having battled with my weight for all of my adult life—and are attracted to low-carb diets but don't want to eat the animal products most of those diets are based on, you need recipes and meal plans that are not only meatless, but are based on principles from diets like the Zone or South Beach.

This cookbook is for you.

*Low-Carb Vegetarian* uses only the best principles from low-carb diets to create nutritious, easy, compassionate, and yummy recipes for anyone—vegetarian or otherwise—who wants to lose weight. The principles are simple: highly processed and carbohydrate-rich foods such as those made with white flour and sugar can increase the appetite, lead to cravings, encourage weight gain, and even promote the incidence of type 2 diabetes. Eliminating or reducing such "bad carbs" as white bread, white rice, white pasta, sugar, fruit juices, and potatoes, while increasing the consumption of vegetables, fruit, soy products, and whole grains, can promote not only short-term weight loss but long-term weight loss and overall health.

I can't promise that you will magically lose dozens of pounds by making the recipes in this book. But I can tell you that if you create a meal plan and diet for yourself based on the principles outlined here, you will feel good about yourself, you'll be eating a diet that's rich in fiber, soy protein, vegetables, and fruits, and you will most likely lose weight. I know I did.

# A Look at Low-Carb Diets

Not all low-carb diets are the same. Some require you to eat a diet based almost entirely on meat products, with carbohydrate counts as low as six grams per meal. For others, the proportion of calories from carbohydrates, proteins, and fats is emphasized. And for still others, carbohydrates only matter at certain times of the day or during certain meals. How do you figure out how to sort through all of the diets and their often conflicting rules? And how do you create a dietary plan that works for you and is nutritious, not too confusing, and will be successful as a long-term eating plan? To help you decide whether a low-carb plan will work for you, we'll start by looking at some of the low-carb diets popular today and the philosophy and science behind them.

## THE LOW-CARB PHILOSOPHY

Low-carb diets differ from traditional diets popular in the United States in that low-carb diets restrict carbohydrates rather than fat or calories. The reason for the focus on carbs rather than calories or fat has to do with the effect that carbohydrates have on the way the body processes sugar.

Simply put, carbohydrates are broken down into glucose during digestion and are released into the bloodstream for fuel. After we eat carbohydrates, our blood glucose (or blood sugar) level rises, giving us a burst of energy. The pancreas, as a reaction to that rise, releases insulin into the bloodstream that allows the sugars to be used by the body. Muscles, fat and other body cells then absorb this insulin, and insulin levels in the blood return to normal.

If a food contains a large quantity of carbohydrates, it can cause a rapid increase in blood sugar, placing a greater burden on the insulin system.

(High-density carbohydrate foods such as breads or cereals contain more carbohydrates than low-density carbohydrate foods such as vegetables.) When the body experiences a rapid rise in blood sugar followed by a surge in insulin, the increased insulin blocks the body's ability to burn stored fuel, causing the body to convert it into fat. This condition is known as insulin resistance—when insulin can no longer properly process fuel—causing the body to store more fat than it should and resulting in weight gain. Further, a rapid rise in blood sugar is always followed by a rapid fall, causing energy levels to drop, concentration to waver, and hunger to increase. Consequently, we crave more carbohydrates to give ourselves another sugar rush, and the cycle continues. Decreasing the consumption of these high-density carbohydrates improves insulin resistance and leads to weight loss rather than fat storage.

Simply put, the faster the sugars and starches we eat are processed and absorbed into the bloodstream, the more we eat and the fatter we get. A diet too high in high-density carbohydrates won't just lead to weight gain, however. The constant elevation of insulin levels can also result in a greater risk for heart disease, type 2 (adult onset) diabetes, and cancer, making the problem more than just cosmetic.

## GOOD CARBS VS. BAD CARBS

This cookbook does not take the position that all carbohydrates are bad carbs. In fact, like nutritionists across the board, I take the opposite position—some foods that are high in carbohydrates should be avoided because of the way that they are processed or the effect that they have on one's blood sugar. But other carbohydrates—most carbs, in fact—should be embraced and should form the majority of a nutritious diet.

"Good" carbohydrates include low-density carbohydrate foods such as vegetables and fruits[2], as well as high-fiber complex carbohydrate foods such as beans and high-fiber breads and cereals.

"Bad" carbs, on the other hand, include many high-density carbohydrate foods such as rice, bread, potatoes, cereal, and pasta. While the complex carbs found in breads provide important nutrients (such as fiber), most of the starchy foods that North Americans eat are made by stripping the fiber from the grain, resulting in nutritionally empty foods that not only increase weight but even increase carbohydrate cravings, according to at least one study. It is these carbohydrates that should be avoided on a low-carb diet.

Another way to understand the difference between good carbs and bad is to learn about the glycemic index. This dietetic tool, introduced by Dr. David Jenkins of the University of Toronto, measures the degree to which eating a particular food increases one's blood sugar and contributes to weight gain. Doctors at the Harvard School of Public Health then developed the concept of glycemic load, which takes into account both a food's glycemic index as well as amount of carbohydrate the food contains.[3] As can be expected from the above discussion, certain starchy foods, such as white bread and potatoes, increase blood sugar faster than other types of foods. For instance, processed breads, baked goods, and cereals carry a glycemic load of 70 to 140, while whole grain, high-fiber cereals, and grains have counts as low as 27. Using the glycemic index or glycemic load of foods are other ways of gauging which

---

2 Not all vegetables and fruits are the same, however. While carrots, potatoes, sweet potatoes, and yams are good for you, they do raise blood sugar and should be avoided while on a low-carb diet. Some fruits like bananas, while nutritious, are also very high in sugar and should be consumed in very small quantities while on a low-carb diet.

3 To find out the glycemic loads of certain foods, go to www.health.harvard.edu/newsweek to find a table full of common foods.

kinds of foods will have a deleterious effect on one's blood sugar, resulting in weight gain.

## POPULAR LOW-CARB DIETS

While many low-carb diets may be similar, some of them differ greatly. Following is a summary of some of the most popular diets, including Atkins, Carbohydrate Addicts, South Beach, and the Zone.

The Atkins diet, first presented in *Dr. Atkins' Diet Revolution*, is the modern predecessor of all of the low-carb diets,[4] and while controversial, is still what most people think of when they think of "low-carb." When Atkins' book first came out in 1972, it challenged the entire nutritional industry, then primarily focused on cutting calories, and later fat (since fat contains so many calories). Atkins' diet, on the other hand, is high in saturated fats and targets carbohydrates, both high and low density. Over thirty years after the first Atkins book was published, this diet concept has gained popularity, and it continues to be both extraordinarily popular and highly controversial.

Atkins' plan is simple. By reducing one's carbohydrate consumption down to about 5% of daily calories (from about 20 grams per day during induction up to about 90 for maintenance), the body goes into an abnormal metabolic state known as ketosis. Without enough carbohydrates, there is not enough glucose available to fuel the body's cells, so fat stores are burned for energy, leading to weight loss. Ketosis refers to the high levels of ketones (the byproducts of fat metabolism) that are present in the blood when this is occurring. Because ketones are eliminated in urine, the presence of ketones can be detected through the use of urine test strips, which dieters use to confirm that they are indeed burning fat. Unfortunately, ketosis, as a permanent body con-

---

4 Many people don't realize that the first known book advocating a low-carb diet was William Banting's *Letter on Corpulence, Addressed to the Public,* published in 1863.

dition, can lead to the loss of electrolytes such as potassium, a loss of muscle mass, dehydration, and metabolic acidosis, while new research suggests that continued ketosis causes oxidation of the lipoproteins, a major contributor to heart disease. Furthermore, many nutritionists believe that a permanent state of ketosis forces the body to adapt to a state of "starvation," holding on to its fat stores for protection.

The greatest problem with the Atkins diet, however, is twofold. First, the diet is extremely high in animal proteins, which, due to their saturated fat content, are a major factor in high cholesterol, colon and prostate cancer, and heart disease, especially when the remainder of the diet is low in fiber. The extraordinarily high level of protein itself can also damage the kidneys and lead to osteoporosis. And second, by eliminating or so strictly curbing the consumption of nutritious carbohydrates such as vegetables, fruits, and whole grains, Atkins dieters miss the well-documented, cancer-fighting health benefits of those foods.

The Zone diet, popularized in Barry Sears' book by the same name, is a much more balanced approach to the concept of low-carb eating. In fact, the entire premise of the diet is balance. According to Dr. Sears, the consumption of certain foods in specific percentages can alter hormone levels and drastically affect health. The goal of the Zone program is to have one's diet hormonally balanced, which means keeping one's hormones within a defined zone; they should never be too high, nor too low. Getting "into the zone" means that by balancing the foods we eat, our hormonal systems will be balanced, which, according to Sears, can extend the lifespan, prevent obesity, and avert chronic disease, as well as allowing better energy, focus, and concentration. The balance that Zone practitioners shoot for is to have 40% of their daily calories derive from carbohydrates, 30% from protein, and 30% from fat.

The rules are relatively simple. Dieters must eat a balance of protein, carbohydrates, and fat at every meal to maintain steady insulin levels and to curb cravings. (While it is the balance of carbohydrate and protein that is critical, fat is also important because it slows down the processing of carbohydrates, and it also is filling and satisfying.) Sears recommends that adherents plan their meals by picking low-density carbohydrates and eating twice as many of those foods than protein, topped with a little bit of fat such as salad dressing.

Portions in the Zone are also controlled, with meals averaging about 300 to 400 calories, and a daily calorie intake of about 1,200 to 1,400 calories. Sears recommends frequent meals and snacks, with every single meal and snack having the same carbohydrate/protein/fat balance of 40/40/30. Finally, Sears limits the amount of protein as well, pointing out that if we eat too much protein, the excess will be converted to fat, because the body can't store excess protein.

The Zone is the only low-carb diet that specifically caters to vegetarians, through Sears' book, the *Soy Zone*. This book combines the balanced low-carb perspective of the Zone with a soy-based vegan diet, resulting in the only ready-made plan that I've seen that can be easily used by vegetarians. However, I feel the recipes in the *Soy Zone* are quite boring, and Sears doesn't include any whole grains in his program at all, leaving the diet quite low in fiber.

The Carbohydrate Addicts program, promoted by Richard and Rachael Heller, takes as its basic premise that some people are addicted to carbohydrates. The diet's response to this problem is unique, however. Adherents of the Carbohydrate Addict's diet strictly restrict carbohydrates throughout the day, but allow themselves a single "reward" meal per day which consists of as many starchy, high-density carbohydrates as can be eaten in an hour, as long as an equal amount of low-density carbs and proteins are consumed at the same time. In other words, you can eat a huge dish of pasta as long as you eat just as much salad and protein along with the pasta. The rest of the day can only include protein and vegetables. If you really feel the need to eat high-density carbs, this may be a diet for you.

According to Arthur Agatston's book *The South Beach Diet*, the optimal nutritional program is not a low-carb diet. But like the Zone, South Beach advocates a reliance on "good" carbs (fruits, vegetables, and whole grains) and a reduction in "bad" carbs, which include rice, pasta, potatoes, white flour, sugar, and fruit juice (primarily foods which have been stripped of fiber during manufacturing). The South Beach program begins with a strict two-week induction period that strictly curbs even normally allowed carbs, such as fruit and alcohol. After two weeks, the program relaxes to the extent that certain foods, such as whole grain bread, can be re-introduced into the diet, albeit in relatively small quantities. Like Atkins and the other diets, though, the South Beach program relies heavily on animal proteins, combined with good carbs, to supply protein.

South Beach has very few strict rules, and there is no counting of calories or carbs. Instead, practitioners simply remember what foods to avoid in what phase and what foods to emphasize. Agatston is critical of the high fat found in the Atkins approach and encourages the consumption of a great deal of vegetables, as well as some high-fiber foods. All of the recipes in this cook-book adhere to the South Beach plan, so if you are attracted to the simplicity of this program, you'll be able to use this book without a problem.

Other low-carb diets include Neanderthin, Sugar Busters, Schwarzbein Principle, and Protein Power. All advocate an avoidance of carbohydrates to a greater or lesser degree, but space limitations don't permit a full discussion of those diets. (See *The Low-Carb Bible* for a nice summary of all the major low-carb diet plans.)

## THE SCIENCE: PRO AND CON

Low-carb diets are as controversial as they are popular. As we've seen, the Atkins diet is very high in animal protein and saturated fat, and dangerously low in vegetables and whole grains. The Neanderthin diet (based on the creator's assumption of how our hunter-gatherer ancestors ate) is even worse. By eliminating or radically reducing these nutritious carbohydrates from one's diet, there is an increased risk of colon and prostate cancers as well as heart disease, hypertension, and stroke, and the huge amounts of protein can damage the kidneys and impact bone density.

On the other hand, elevated insulin levels associated with diets heavy in high-density carbohydrates have been associated with breast, stomach, and colon cancers, as well as type 2 diabetes. One recent study points to a correlation between a diet with a high glycemic load and colorectal cancer. In addition, recent studies have shown that low-carb diets do lead to at least short-term weight loss, with no yet-documented negative effects on dieters' health.[5]

So how do you decide whether a low-carb diet is safe, nutritious, and will work? Fortunately, the vast majority of the negative reviews of low-carbohydrate diets from nutritionists and others are aimed at Atkins and other programs that radically reduce all carbohydrates and replace them with high lev-

---

5 Recent studies include two clinical trials whose results were published in the *New England Journal of Medicine* in May 2003, which showed that these diets did result in at least short-term weight loss and did not result in an increase of blood cholesterol. These studies are, like the Atkins program itself, very controversial. Some of the most recent studies, like the Durham Veterans Administration Medical Center study led by Dr. Eric Westman, were funded by the Atkins Center. Others are very preliminary,

els of animal protein and fat. For example, the Physicians Committee for Responsible Medicine has been one of the major opponents of low-carb diets; yet their critique is focused on the heavy use of meat and fat in the Atkins diet, along with the loss of vegetables and grains.

Moderate programs like the Zone and South Beach, with their emphasis on vegetables, some fruits, and whole grains, have not been the focus of these nutritional critiques. Further, by combining a moderate low-carb approach such as the Zone or South Beach with a vegetarian diet, we can expect to reap all of the benefits of low-carb diets—balanced insulin and blood sugar levels, steady and controlled weight loss, and a boost to energy and focus—along with the well-known benefits of a vegetarian diet, rich in cancer-fighting vegetables and whole grains.

## How Many Carbs is Low-Carb?

When many of us hear the term "low-carb," we think of the extreme version of low-carb most typically thought of as Atkins: a diet filled with meat and animal fat, lacking in vegetables, grains, and beans, with carb counts as low as 20 grams per day, or 5 or 6 grams per meal.

That's not what this cookbook is about and not what I mean by low-carb. My working assumption is that carbs are not by themselves bad, but that too many refined carbohydrates increase weight and need to be curbed. In addition, the fact that vegetables, beans, and whole grains *are* primarily carbs, yet have been proven to be nutritious from every angle, means that it doesn't make sense to eliminate or even severely restrict them.

---

and still others have methodologies that are being questioned by other researchers. None of these studies follow participants for longer than a couple of years. Finally, many researchers note that it's actually decreased calorie consumption, rather than lower carbohydrate consumption, that has led to the weight loss seen in many of these studies.

You'll find recipes in this book that are based on vegetables, fruits, beans, and some grains, combined with soy-based proteins. Because of the prevalence of these foods in my recipes, the carb counts will range from as low as 4 grams to as high as 50 grams in each recipe.[6] You'll want to choose recipes that have carb counts that fit with the weight loss program and phase that you are using. Hopefully your new lifestyle will be a long term or permanent lifestyle, and if so, you'll need a variety of recipes with a range of healthful carb counts to take you from your induction phase through your weight loss period and on to your years of maintenance.

Because many of the recipes in this book include foods filled with health-promoting fiber such as beans, which are relatively high in carbs, you may find that the carb count in particular recipes is higher than others; one count is as high as 72 grams. This brings up a concept that some people call "net carbs" and others call the "effective carb count."

Fiber is a carbohydrate, but it is a carbohydrate that is not absorbed by the body. Ingesting fiber will not increase one's blood sugar or release insulin; it will slow the absorption of starches and sugars into the body. Eating carbs that are rich in fiber is not only beneficial to one's health, but is an important factor in a low-carb diet. Because of fiber's benefits, many low-carb dieters and diet advocates subtract fiber grams from carb grams to determine the "net carb" count of a food or recipe. You'll see that I've done this in a few of my recipes that are especially rich in fiber.

---

6 As a comparison, food industry groups and consumer groups are currently petitioning the FDA to release guidelines on what is a "low-carb" food. For instance, the Grocery Manufacturers of America is asking for a definition of 9 grams of carbs per serving while the Center for Science in the Public Interest is asking for 6 grams per serving.

## The Role of Fat and Fiber in a Low-Carb Diet

But what about fat? Common sense tells us that eating too much fat will make us fat. Each gram of fat translates to 9 calories (as opposed to only 4 for protein and 4 for carbohydrates), so it makes sense to assume that by eating too many fats one will gain weight, and research has indeed shown this to be true. Additionally, certain fats, such as saturated fats found in meats and butter, and trans fats (a type of artificial polyunsaturated fat found in commercially made cakes, cookies, and margarines) have been found to lead to cardiovascular disease, heart attack, and stroke. Yet for many Americans, a low-fat diet does not result in weight loss—especially when that diet is based heavily on prepackaged "low-fat" foods that often are extremely high in calories, refined carbohydrates, and unhealthful fat substitutes.

When nutritionists first released their recommendations advocating a low-fat diet, most of the fats consumed by Americans were saturated fats, which do indeed contribute to clogged arteries and increase one's risk for heart attack and stroke. At that time, not much was known about unsaturated fats such as olive oil, peanut oil, and canola oil, or nuts and avocados, which studies now show can reduce the risk of heart attack or stroke.

It is true that since fats contain more calories than carbohydrates or protein, eating too much fat will lead to weight gain. But eating moderate amounts of fat within a low-carb diet can be beneficial for health in a number of ways. First, eating fats leaves us satisfied. Because of this, many of us would eat fewer calories as fats than we would eat as carbohydrates that raise blood sugar levels, cause us to become hungry quickly, and lead to overeating and weight gain.

Second, fat works to inhibit weight gain in another way. As we've discussed, the faster the sugars and starches we eat are processed and absorbed into the bloodstream, the more weight we will gain, so anything that will slow down the process by which the body digests carbs is beneficial. Both the South Beach and the Zone programs promote eating both fiber and fat with carbohydrates, because both of these nutrients slow the digestion of carbs and the absorption of sugar into the bloodstream. This is why the Zone, in particular, advocates eating fat with every meal, because not only does fat not cause a rise in blood sugar levels the way that carbs do, it works to slow the processing of the carbohydrates.

Fiber, like fat, plays an important role in a healthy low-carb diet, although unlike fat, it is largely absent from the Atkins plan as well as other popular low-carb programs. Fiber is a complex carbohydrate but is unique among nutrients in that the body can't break it down during digestion. It's important for a number of reasons: it aids digestion, deters heart disease and cancer, and it fills you up, leaving less room in the stomach for other foods. Unlike high-density carbs, though, it doesn't promote a craving for carbs soon after consuming it. Fiber is especially useful for low-carb dieters because eating fiber with other carbs slows the release of glucose into the bloodstream, preventing insulin surges that can result in weight gain. Fiber-rich foods put the stomach to work; the greater the fiber content, the slower the absorption of sugar and the slower the release of insulin. This is why most low-carb diets recommend eating whole fruits rather than fruit juice; you will reap the same nutritional benefits from fruit as from fruit juice, but because of the fiber, the fruit will be absorbed much more slowly than the fruit juice, leading to a slower release of insulin and less of an impact on blood sugar levels. Finally, because the body cannot digest fiber, it does not "count" as a calorie, and because fiber slows the absorption of sugars into the system, it even reduces the impact of the carbs that you do eat.

## How Much Protein?

All of the low-carb diets discussed in this book are higher in protein than the typical vegetarian diet, although not necessarily higher than the meat-based American diet. For these diets, vegetarians do need to eat more protein than they may be used to, but we still shouldn't eat too much.

Recent research does point to the health benefits, particularly for women, of eating protein. One study from Harvard Medical School suggests that the more protein women consume, the less likely they are to develop heart disease. Another study found that the more protein women consume, the fewer hip fractures they suffer. Still other research suggests that increasing protein increases weight loss, as well as increasing breast cancer patients' chance of survival.

However, we can still consume too much protein. One problem with the very high protein amounts required of the Atkins diet is that the body cannot store excess protein. If you eat more protein than the body needs, the excess protein will be turned into fat.

So how much is too much? The Zone recommends that followers never eat any more protein in one meal than can fit in the palm of a hand. That's where the Zone's recommendation of 75 to 100 grams per day comes from (or 20 to 30 grams per meal). Protein counts in this book range anywhere from very low (for salads and several soups intended to be side dishes) to anywhere from 7 grams to as high as 30 grams—well within the range of the Zone and South Beach.

This cookbook includes soy as the basis for the protein in most of the recipes. There are a number of reasons for this. While most vegetarians today know that vegetables contain protein (and no longer have to be combined to achieve "complete" protein, as was assumed in the early '70s), soybeans are the only vegetable that contains more protein than carbohydrate, making them perfect for the vegetarian who wants to control their carbs. Additionally, soy contains isoflavones, which are disease-fighting substances found only in plants. Studies show that soy isoflavones can decrease cholesterol levels, may ward off a variety of diseases ranging from heart disease to cancer to osteoporosis, and can even alleviate many menopausal discomforts.

Unlike 25 years ago when I became a vegetarian, today there are hundreds of soy-based products on the market, so none of us need to grind our own soybeans, make our own soymilk, or create our own soy burgers (unless we want to). Today, anyone can buy a wide variety of burgers, bacon, sausages, hot dogs, chicken- or fish-style cutlets, and almost any other meat analog—all at the local chain supermarket. Best of all, these products are lower in fat than those made of meat, contain all the documented benefits of soy, and are easily adapted to the low-carb lifestyle.

## Why do Vegetarians Need a Low-Carb Diet?

If you're a vegetarian with a weight problem, you've probably heard the following not-very-polite comment: "But I thought vegetarians were skinny." It is widely assumed that because vegetarians eat little or no animal protein they should be thinner than those whose protein choices are much higher in fat. But that is not always the case.

The problem with the traditional vegetarian diet is that it relies heavily on grains and starches. In today's world, these are primarily processed grains and starches that are very high in carbohydrates, raise blood sugar levels too quickly, and cause insulin levels to soar. As we've seen earlier, this surge is followed by a rapid plunge in blood sugar, causing us to feel sluggish and hungry for more carbohydrate-heavy food. On top of that, many vegetarians fall into the same junk food trap that other Americans do—eating chips, cookies, candies, and breads, all of which are high not only in carbohydrates but also fat and calories. A vegetarian or even vegan diet alone is not enough to assure weight control.

I am an example. I've been a vegetarian for over 25 years, but I have struggled with my weight all of my adult life. Like a lot of people, I'm an emotional eater, and I eat to deal with stress. But I don't just eat. I eat unhealthfully—a lot of fried foods, a lot of snacks, and a huge amount of sweets. And even though I'm a vegetarian, for many years I ate very few vegetables (unless they were deep fried) and hardly any fruit.

A couple of years ago my life became so stressful that I was eating all the time, and my weight finally topped 200 pounds. Even though I was jogging a couple of days a week, I was so heavy that my legs hurt, my back hurt, and my feet hurt terribly. Something had to be done.

Over the years, I tried all kinds of diets, but none ever stuck. Like a lot of people, I would lose weight and then gain it right back later—generally in higher quantities than the weight I originally lost. Obviously, a traditional diet would not solve my problem, but a serious change in my lifestyle was necessary—I needed to deal with the emotional roots of my eating, but I also needed to learn to eat more nutritious foods, not just for the duration of a diet, but forever.

About a year ago, my sister told me about the Zone (which I knew was a low-carb diet favored by many Hollywood celebrities) and mentioned that there was a vegan version of the diet, called the Soy Zone, as well. I figured I couldn't lose anything, so I bought the book and decided to give it a shot.

Without sounding like a magazine ad, I have to say I couldn't believe the results. In six months, I lost 45 pounds, and I felt 100% better. I was able to walk and run without pain, I dropped to a size 12 (not seen for years), and gained a huge amount of self-confidence. To top it all off, I found a new way of eating that was more healthful, easy to manage, included lots of vegetables, and eliminated foods that I could, it turns out, live without.

On the other hand, the program, if it was to be a lifelong program and not just a diet, needed to have enough variety in it to keep me from being bored. I still look forward to eating as much as I always did, so if there's nothing good to look forward to, a meal plan becomes much harder to stick with, and I start to thumb through the take-out menus again. You just can't eat tofu dogs and vegetables every night of the week.

That's why I wrote this book. I wanted to find recipes that were tasty, interesting, creative, easy to prepare, and that were low-carb enough to meet the standards of the Zone, South Beach, or other healthful low-carb diets. I figured if I lost weight with this approach and needed to find enough recipes to keep me satisfied and interested, then other vegetarians would too.

I hope this book helps you with your own weight control program and leads to a healthier, happier lifestyle.

# The Vegetarian Low-Carb Plan

The eating plan advocated in this book is simple. It eliminates all processed, refined, high-density carbohydrates like white pasta, bread, rice, baked goods, cereals, and foods with sugar and other natural sweeteners, as well as several extra high-density vegetables like carrots and potatoes. It replaces those products with a wide variety of low-density carbohydrates, drawing from almost every vegetable, most fruits, and many whole grains. And finally, it includes a reasonable amount of soy protein, as well as a moderate amount of fat. Meals are, for the most part, easy to create and based on the above principles. The recipes in this book are derived from a number of ethnic cuisines and emphasize spices and flavor. Here's how to get started.

## THE LOW-CARB VEGETARIAN KITCHEN

To be successful with any long-term eating plan, you'll need to create an environment of success. In the case of moving to a low-carbohydrate diet, that means eliminating high carbohydrate and processed foods from your kitchen and replacing them with vegetables, whole grains, and lots of soy products.

Things to toss out

* White rice, flour, pasta, and bread. Even "wheat" bread and brown rice aren't whole grain enough and are too full of high-density, high-glycemic carbohydrates, so don't let the packages fool you![7]

---

7 "Wheat bread" usually contains a mixture of white flour, which has much of the wheat stripped away, and whole wheat flour, with as much as 75% being white in many breads. On the other hand, breads labeled as "whole wheat" or "whole grain" bread will be composed of the entire wheat kernel, leaving it much higher in fiber and good nutrients.

* Anything made with white flour, such as cakes, cookies, and muffins
* Low-fiber cereals and sweetened cereals
* Anything with sugar, honey, corn syrup, or any other natural sweetener
* Potatoes, sweet potatoes, carrots, corn, and yams
* Tortillas, both flour and corn
* Chips of all kinds
* Fruit juice (except for limited use)
* Nondiet sodas

Foods to stock

Now that you have eliminated all of the non-nutritious temptations in your kitchen, it's time to go shopping! Here are some foods you'll want to purchase:

* *Tofu: silken, soft, firm, and extra firm.* I buy a lot of tofu and you should too! The general rule is the firmer the tofu, the higher the protein level, but don't let that lead you to believe that you shouldn't buy the soft varieties too. Silken tofu, in particular, gives good results in recipes that call for blending, such as ice creams, puddings, and creamy soups.

* *Prepared tofu: marinated, braised, or baked tofu.* These are good for snacks and sandwiches and are found in the deli section of the grocery store.

* *Beans.* I buy canned beans because I'm too lazy to soak and boil beans for hours. But they are certainly less expensive when dry, so if you want to feel extra virtuous about your beans, feel free to buy them that way. Just remember to prepare them well in advance of cooking.

* *Textured soy protein.* This is a dehydrated meat substitute found in many natural food stores, as well as online, that can be added to sauces and soups to give extra protein and fiber.

*Meat substitutes:*

* *Hamburger crumbles.* Morningstar Farms, Yves, and other companies make this product, which can be found in the deli section or the freezer. Burger crumbles can be used whenever ground beef or turkey is called for.

* *Cold cuts.* Yves and Tofurky each make really tasty sandwich slices, and new varieties are coming out all the time.

* *Seitan* is a very high-protein meat substitute made from wheat (gluten). You can use it in stews and other dishes where chunks of meat might normally be used, and it can substitute for tofu in many recipes as well.

* *Chicken or fish substitutes.* Morningstar Farms and Garden Burger make varieties of these products. Avoid breaded cutlets, though, because the breading obviously adds on unwanted carbs.

* *Tofu dogs.* Tofu dogs and veggie dogs are easy to find in any grocery store and are a fast meal option. Check the labels as some have a higher carb count than others.

* *Soy burgers.* Morningstar Farms, Garden Burger, Boca Burger, and Yves all make delicious soy burgers. Check the ingredients, though, because some of them may have dairy in them, and others are relatively high in carbohydrates.

*Sausages and bacon.* Yves, Morningstar Farms, and Tofurky all make different varieties of bacon and sausage, which are great for both breakfasts as well as main dishes. Again, check the ingredients to make sure they meet your needs.

*Other ingredients*

* *Soy protein powder* for extra protein. This can be purchased in the bulk section of a natural foods store or in big containers in the diet section of supermarkets. The brand I use is Andronico's, vanilla flavored, with a scoop size

of 28 grams. Each scoop contains 110 calories, 1 gram of fat, no carbohydrates, and 24 grams of protein. If the brand of protein powder that you buy has different amounts of the above nutrients, simply adjust the quantities you use accordingly.

* *Soy flour.* I didn't include any baked goods in this cookbook, but if you decide to try your hand at baking low-carbohydrate breads, cakes, or cookies, you'll want to use soy flour instead of wheat flour, and I do use soy flour in some savory dishes for thickening. If you do decide to bake with soy flour, you'll only be able to replace about a quarter of the wheat flour with soy flour, as soy flour does not bind ingredients the way wheat does.

* *Soy yogurt* (unflavored) for smoothies and other breakfast dishes. Soy yogurt is also another way to add creaminess to savory dishes, such as stroganoff. Sweetened soy yogurts or those with fruit in them will be much higher in carbs than plain varieties. If you like a fruity yogurt, just buy plain soy yogurt and add vanilla and fresh fruit to it.

* *Soy mayonnaise.* There are a number of brands of this available on the market. Check both the mayonnaise aisle and also the deli section where tofu and other soy products are located. Remember that fat and calorie counts (although not carb counts) differ greatly sometimes with these products, so you may want to read a couple of labels before bringing some home.

* *Whole grain bread.* Here again you need to read the ingredients to find out which breads are the high-protein, low-carb, low-fiber breads you're looking for. We use exclusively Alvarado Street Bakery breads in my household, all of which have carb counts as low as 10 grams per slice, protein as high as 6 grams per slice, and about 70 calories and at least 2 grams of fiber apiece. (Atkins and other low-carb companies make low-carb breads; while they're

low-carb, you'll find that many are very high in calories and fat, and very low in fiber.)

* *High-fiber and high-protein cereals.* I have a list later in the book of the kinds of cereals to stock. You'll want to purchase cereals with either a high level of fiber or a high protein count, as well as a low-carbohydrate count. Again, Atkins makes a low-carb cereal, but I'm not satisfied with the flavor. Better to stick with the traditional brands of cereal that are naturally low-carb, and very high in fiber.

* *Soy pasta.* I didn't include a lot of pasta recipes in this cookbook, because I think it's safer to cut down on the amount of pasta in one's diet, rather than relying on it as a staple the way many vegetarians do. But there are some good low-carb and high-protein pastas on the market today. I don't like the taste of the Atkins brand pastas, but I love the angel hair, spaghetti, and fettuccine made by Soy Deli. These are found in the deli case of good supermarkets and each serving contains just 18 carbs and a whopping 14 grams of protein.

* *Splenda (sucralose).* This is the artificial sugar that I use for all of my desserts and a few of the other recipes that call for a sweetener. It's made from real sugar, so it tastes the most like sugar of any artificial sweeteners I've tried.

* *Vegetable bouillon cubes or powder.* These are easy to use and are found in the soup aisle of the grocery store.

* *Soymilk* is now found in any grocery store and comes in plain, vanilla, and chocolate varieties. Sadly, chocolate soymilk is too high in carbs to be used by folks on a low-carb diet, but you can make your own by adding unsweetened cocoa powder and Splenda to your plain or vanilla soymilk.

* *Vegetables of all kinds.* We buy so many vegetables per week that we barely have room for them in the refrigerator. But the upside is that I know my

diet is more healthful than it ever was before I went on a low-carb diet. Again, avoid potatoes, yams, sweet potatoes, carrots, and corn, as they all carry a high glycemic load.

* *Fruits of all kinds.* Try to eat fruit every day, in place of fruit juices, and also as a regular part of your diet. Some fruits—bananas in particular—are very high in carbs so should be eaten in small quantities.

* *Nuts and nut butters.* Nuts are a great low-carb snack, although they should be eaten in moderation because of their high fat content. On the other hand, substituting nuts, nut butters, olives, or avocadoes for oils in recipes can be helpful for dieters as they fill you up more than oils and provide protective antioxidants. Look for nut butters that are unsweetened.

* *Oils.* Buy olive and canola oils for cooking and for salads, and sesame and peanut oils for stir-frys and other Asian dishes. Stay away from polyunsaturated vegetable fats such as soybean, sunflower, safflower, and corn oils, as they are higher in omega-6 fatty acids, which can be damaging to the heart. And avoid margarine and most other solid vegetable fats. They contain trans fatty acids, which are as harmful to heart health as saturated fats from animal products.

* *Popcorn.* Popcorn is a relatively low-carb snack, so you should keep some around the house for video nights.

I do not recommend that you purchase a great deal of low-carb specialty products, such as Atkins food products, even though they are indeed very low-carb. Many of these products replace carbohydrates with fat (often dangerous hydrogenated fat), making them less than nutritious and very high in calories. Many others are stripped of fiber, as are so many prepackaged food products. It is my feeling that, except for the soy meat substitutes, tofu, and several other ingredients found in my recipes, a low-carb diet is much more nutritious when based primarily on whole foods rather than packaged foods. Packaged low-carb products also tend to be much more expensive than whole foods, and many (such as the salad dressings) are only marginally lower in carbohydrates than standard products, at a much greater cost.

If you do want to try some of these pastas, bread mixes, food bars, or snacks, remember that it's not just the carb count that matters. Read the entire food label to see what you are buying before making your purchase.

The same advice holds for eating out. Today, many restaurants are touting their new "low-carb menus." For the most part, these should be avoided. Most are based primarily on meat and cheese, and consumer groups have shown that the low-carb meals promoted by fast food restaurants (as well as sit down restaurants) are extraordinarily high in fat and calories. Eating out as a vegetarian on a low-carb diet does not have to be impossible, however. Aim for restaurants that offer tofu dishes and choose tofu and vegetable meals without the rice or pasta. Although some of their dishes can also be high in fat, Chinese and Thai restaurants are a good bet for the low-carb vegetarian.

Finally, what about alcohol? Alcohol is not a carbohydrate; it's created when the sugars in beer, wine, and liquor ferment. Alcohol per se does not raise blood sugar, so it doesn't affect the body the way that carbohydrates do. On the other hand, because of the way that they're processed, some alcoholic beverages (like beer) do have carbs in them, and all alcohols have calories—seven calories per gram (as compared to four for a carbohydrate).

So can you include alcohol, in limited quantities, in a low-carb diet? Yes and no. While there are low-carb beers on the market today, and alcohols like vodka or gin have no carbs at all, they do, as mentioned, have calories. In addition, alcohol actually slows down a diet because the body reacts to the presence of alcohol by burning it before other kinds of fuel. That's why many diets recommend no alcohol at all during the induction phase of the diet, and only limited alcohol after that.

## USEFUL APPLIANCES

You won't need fancy appliances to cook the recipes in this book. However, there are a few tools that will make cooking much easier for you, and more fun too.

* *Food processor.* I never knew how useful a food processor was until I started making a lot of the blended dishes that you'll find in this cookbook. While a blender can work, a food processor is tailored to mixing more than just drinks and, for the most part, will work better for you than a blender. Go with what works for you, depending on the quality of your blender and/or food processor. If you find that your food processor isn't making certain mixtures (such as those containing tofu) completely smooth, combine your mixture with a wire whisk or large spoon, and blend in batches in your blender. Combine the batches by hand when you're finished.

* *Small kitchen scale.* There's something about a food scale that screams "diet." I remember my mother measuring foods on a scale when I was young, and it seemed like the saddest thing to have to measure all of your foods. However, if you've never really prepared foods and eaten mindfully before, you may not actually know much about serving sizes, and a scale is a useful tool to help you to understand how much of something you're actually eating. A scale can also be very useful when you cook with tofu. Tofu is difficult to measure in cups, and all of my recipes measure tofu by ounces and pounds. If the tofu you buy comes in blocks that are less than a pound (or aren't always the same weight), it can be difficult to estimate the amount to use in

a recipe. On the other hand, if the tofu you buy comes in standard one-pound packages, you can more easily see how to divide the blocks into quarters (for 4 ounces), halves (for 8 ounces), or three quarters (for 12 ounces).

* *Good knives.* This seems self evident, but if you haven't cooked much until now, you may not recognize that the knives you use to do everything from cut food to open the pickle jar can't even cut a tomato anymore. So invest in a couple of good knives and learn how to sharpen them. You'll find your job in the kitchen is much easier and safer.

* *Ice cream maker.* If you want to make the ice creams and sorbets in this book, you'll need to get one of these. But don't worry. Today's ice cream makers are nothing like the big wooden contraption your family had when you were a kid, where you had to sit in the bathtub surrounded by rock salt and crank till you got tennis elbow. Today's makers are nifty little devices in which you keep the freezer bowl in the freezer until you're ready, and all it takes is a few cranks in front of the TV to get your ice cream. Ours is by Donvier.

* *Vegetable chopper.* I'm almost embarrassed to mention something that is mostly seen in late night infomercials or ads in the backs of tabloids. But these things work! Ours is a bright lime green machine made by Zyliss, and we use it almost exclusively to mince things: from onions to garlic to ginger to mushrooms to herbs. It saves you a lot of slicing, and the sound of the chopper on the cutting board is kind of neat. If you want to buy one, you'll want to look for a chopper that has a very sharp blade, a nice spring loaded mechanism, and a comfortable plunger, since that's what you will be handling as you chop your vegetables. Make sure also that the chopper has a safety mechanism so that the blades can never cut you or anyone else.

* *Good measuring cups and spoons.* This also seems obvious, but if you're not a regular cook or just throw things into the pot willy-nilly, you'll really need a set of measuring cups and spoons to measure your ingredients, at least until you get familiar with the recipes.

* *Nonstick saucepans.* These are useful if you're trying to reduce the fat in your diet and don't want to use much oil for sautéing.

## HOW TO WORK WITH TOFU

You'll be using a lot of tofu when making the recipes in this book, so it's helpful to know a couple of tips on working with tofu before you get started.

* *Draining.* Tofu often comes packaged in vacuum-sealed containers filled with water, and the tofu itself retains a lot of moisture. You'll want to drain the tofu before cooking with it. You can set your tofu in a strainer or on several paper towels, and if you're in a hurry, place something heavy on top to help press out the water.

* *Storage.* If you have leftover uncooked tofu, store it in a tightly closed container with fresh water, and change the water daily. Fresh tofu out of its vacuum pack will usually last only a week in the refrigerator, even when the water is changed frequently, so remember to use it up quickly.

* *Freezing and thawing.* Frozen firm tofu has a completely different texture that many people like—it's chewier and absorbs more of the flavors of sauces or marinades than fresh tofu. Simply freeze an unopened tub of tofu in your freezer. Thaw at room temperature or in the microwave, and press to remove the excess water before using in a recipe.

* *Blending.* I prefer silken tofu in recipes requiring a creamy texture, such as desserts and soups. (Check the previous section on food processors and blenders to get more tips for blending tofu.) Before blending cooked foods

with tofu, be sure they are completely cooled to keep from cooking the tofu in your blender or processor. Generally, try to use the type of tofu (regular or silken) the recipes call for. If you only have access to the firmer regular tofu when making recipes calling for silken tofu, try processing it in a blender to get the smoothest results.

* *Crumbles.* Recipes like Tofu Scramble on pages 46 to 47 call for crumbling tofu into a pan and typically sautéing with vegetables in oil.

* *Cubes.* Some of the recipes in this book call for slicing the tofu into cubes and adding them into a sauce; others call for sautéing or even deep-frying tofu cubes.

# How to Put the Plan in Action

You can use this book whether or not you have committed to a specific low-carb diet. If you're on the Zone, you'll need to watch carb counts but especially the percentages of carbs vs. protein and fat. For the other diets, you may be aiming at a specific carb count per meal or per day. You can use the counts for each recipe in this book and put together your meal plans from there.

If, on the other hand, you just want to cut down on your carbs, you can eat any of the recipes in the book, in almost any combination that you want, and you'll find that your carb count will stay in the region of the moderate low-carb diets. If you're trying to do Atkins or the induction phase of South Beach, you'll have a little harder time, as most of my recipes are not that extreme. But there are some recipes that will work for you as well, although I don't recommend Atkins as a long-term approach.

No matter what diet you're on, if you follow these recipes and later modify your own favorite recipes keeping the basic rules of low-carb eating in mind (no white flour, bread, rice, pasta, tortillas; no sugar or honey; no fruit juice; no starchy vegetables like potatoes or corn), you will be eating a diet rich in vegetables and soy, low in "bad" carbohydrates, and one that will keep you satisfied. Snacks and desserts should follow the plan as well.

In general, most of the diets recommend that you eat about five times per day so you never feel hungry, and this makes good sense to me. In addition, you will be eating a variety of vegetables, soy protein products, and some whole grains. How many of each should you eat per day, and what should be your goal in terms of carbs, calories, and the like? A simple guideline to follow might be to eat:

*10 to 15 servings of vegetables and fruits*

A typical serving of fruit = 1 apple, ½ cup cut-up fruit

A typical serving of vegetables = 1 cup of raw leafy vegetables or ½ cup of diced raw or cooked vegetables

*2 to 3 whole grains such as whole grain cereal and whole grain bread*

A typical serving of grain = 1 slice whole grain bread, ½ to 1 cup of cereal, or ½ cup of cooked pasta

*60 to 100 grams protein every day of which at least two servings consist of soy products (aim for the higher end if on the Zone or South Beach).*

One serving of tofu = 6 to 8 ounces tofu (⅜ to ½ of a pound) which will yield anywhere from 10 to 21 grams of protein, depending on how dense or firm the tofu is.

One serving of beans = ½ cup of beans, yielding 6 grams of protein.

* No more than 150 grams carbs every day

* 25 to 35 grams fiber every day

* If you're on the Zone, you'll need to always balance proteins (30%), carbs (40%) and fat (30%).

* Approximately 50 to 60 grams fat every day, or no more than 30%-40% of daily calories

* Calorie counts of about 400 per meal or 1,400 per day

*Watch portion sizes.* Once you can easily recognize a serving size, it will be harder to overeat. Use everyday objects to visualize portion size. The palm of your hand or a deck of cards should equal a serving of protein; a clenched fist or a tennis ball should equal a serving of fruit or nonleafy vegetables; a golf ball should equal a serving of nuts; a die should approximate a serving of fat; and a computer mouse can approximate a serving of healthy grains.

Remember that if you're creating your own meals and meal plans, and if you want to figure out calorie counts, you need to:

*Multiply the carb grams times 4 to get the total calories from carbs
(and to figure the percentage),*

*Multiply protein grams by 4 to get the total calories from protein,*

*Multiply fat grams by 9 to get the total calories from fat.*

If you're not on the Zone and aren't concerned about keeping protein levels balanced with carbs, you can still follow the recipes outlined in this book, but you don't need to use as much protein as is called for in some of the recipes. The general principles should remain: avoid all processed carbs. If you're on the South Beach Diet Phase One, you'll skip all fruits and grains, but after the first two weeks, you'll add those back in again. It is not recommended to continue with such a strict plan for longer than two weeks.

Even if you're not on the Zone or South Beach, it makes sense to combine certain kinds of foods at meals. We want to slow down the processing of carbohydrates in the body, and there are, as discussed earlier, a few methods that accomplish this easily and healthfully. Eating whole foods with lots of fiber means that the sugars produced by the foods are released much more slowly into the system. Combining carbohydrate-rich foods with fat is another way to slow the release of sugars into the body. Whole fiber breads and fruits with skin intact are much better than processed bread or fruits or juices with the fiber removed. Eating protein with carbohydrates is another way to slow the release of sugar into the system, slowing down the body's production of insulin and staving off the inevitable carb cravings.

Finally, if you're not on a specific diet plan, don't worry about the nutritional analyses given in the recipes or making sure that you're keeping your proteins and carbs in balance. As long as you follow the recipes and the principles behind them, you'll find that you're eating a nutritious, satisfying diet that should result in weight loss.

## Meal Plans

The recipes and meal plans in this book follow the principles of the major low-carb diets[8] popular today; they emphasize complex carbohydrates found in most vegetables and fruits, and they reduce or eliminate most simple and refined carbohydrates. While each of the major diets approaches this a little differently, the majority of the meals in this book are appropriate for followers of the two most popular diets outside of Atkins: South Beach (after Phase One) and the Zone.

Followers of the Zone must observe a fairly strict set of rules regarding percentages of carbohydrates to fat and to protein. Zone meals and Zone meal plans should always have the same Zone proportions: 40% carbohydrates, 30% fat, and 30% protein. A typical Zone day will consist of approximately 1,200 calories for a woman and 1,500 for a man. That means that men will need to eat approximately 155 grams of carbohydrates per day, 112 grams of protein, and 50 grams of fat, while women will need to eat 123 grams of carbohydrates per day, 89 grams of protein, and 39 grams of fat.

South Beach meals differ greatly according to whether they are Phase One or Phase Two. During Phase One (which should last only two weeks), carbohydrates are limited to approximately 50 grams per day, with a protein count as high as 150 grams per day. During Phase Two of the diet, carbohydrate intake rises to approximately 150 grams per day and protein drops to 95 grams per day. This puts the diet much closer to the Zone and the other popular programs.

It will be indicated whether the recipes in this book are appropriate for Zone or South Beach Phase One. Many recipes that are not necessarily appropriate for these two diets can be modified to fit them. All fit within the parameters of the basic low-carb approach by emphasizing complex carbohydrates and eliminating most simple or processed carbohydrates.

---

8 Except Atkins and "Neaderthin"

# Three Sample Meal Plans

## DAY ONE

| | |
|---|---|
| *Breakfast:* | Oatmeal with Raspberries, page 44 |
| *Lunch:* | Cream of Mushroom Soup, page 52 with Basic Vegetable Salad, page 80-81 |
| *Snack:* | Mock Lunchmeat Roll Ups, page 132 |
| *Dinner:* | Tofu Miso Soup with Sushi, page 54 |
| *Dessert:* | Strawberry Tofu Sorbet, page 142 |

*Total Count per day:*

Servings: 2 fruits, 8 vegetables, 1 grain, 4 proteins

| | |
|---|---|
| Protein: 67 grams | 20% of calories |
| Carbs: 131 grams | 39% of calories |
| Fat: 65 grams | 43% of calories |
| Calories: 1,352 | Fiber: 20 grams |

## DAY TWO

| | |
|---|---|
| *Breakfast:* | Tofu Scramble with Veggie Bacon, pages 46-47 and piece of fruit |
| *Lunch:* | Spicy Black Bean Soup, page 56-57 with Basic Vegetable Salad, page 80-81 |
| *Snack:* | Deviled Tofu with Celery, page 133 |
| *Dinner:* | "Chicken" Caesar Salad, page 79 |
| *Dessert:* | Chocolate Coconut Mousse, page 145 |

*Total Count per day (Day Two, cont.):*

| Servings: 1 fruit, 9 vegetables, 5 proteins | |
| --- | --- |
| Protein: 66 grams | 19% of calories |
| Carbs: 134 grams | 40% of calories |
| Fat: 63 grams | 42% of calories |
| Calories: 1,347 | Fiber: 29 grams |

## DAY THREE

| | |
| --- | --- |
| *Breakfast:* | Berry Banana Smoothie, page 48 |
| *Lunch:* | Cold Cut Sandwich, page 91 with half serving of Basic Vegetable Salad, page 80-81 |
| *Snack:* | Edamame Quickie Snack, page 134 |
| *Dinner:* | Japanese Salad, page 77 with Tofu in Ginger-Coconut Sauce, page 108-109 |
| *Dessert:* | Coconut Strawberry Pudding, page 146 |

*Total Count per day:*

| Servings: 2 fruit, 9 vegetables, 5 proteins, 2 grain | |
| --- | --- |
| Protein: 74 grams | 21% of calories |
| Carbs: 137 grams | 38% of calories |
| Fat: 65 grams | 41% of calories |
| Calories: 1,425 | Fiber: 32 grams |

# *Breakfast*

Nutritionists have long counseled that we eat a proper breakfast. Starting the day on an empty stomach allows blood sugar to drop, metabolism to slow down, and hunger to increase over the course of the morning. This in turn leads to a lack of energy and focus, as well as almost inevitable midmorning snacking, and for many of us, that means office donuts or the break room snack machine.

Dieters who skip breakfast as a means of saving calories don't realize that they are sabotaging their diets. I know, because I did this for years (I actually skipped breakfast and lunch). I ended up overeating the second I got home from work and often ate all throughout the evening as well.

Starting the morning off with a nutritious breakfast—one that includes good carbohydrates (nonstarchy fruits and vegetables), protein, and fiber-rich foods—not only gives you the energy that you'll need to accomplish your daily goals, but will stave off the inevitable hunger pangs. At least one study even shows that eating "bad" (highly processed) carbs for breakfast caused participants to eat more over the day than those participants who ate a fiber-rich breakfast or one based primarily on protein and vegetables.

All of the recipes in this chapter follow the basic premises of a healthful low-carb diet; they are based on soy protein, fresh fruit or vegetables, and whole grains, and most are appropriate for the Zone and South Beach. The smoothies and cereal options are all very easy to prepare, making them perfect for busy weekday mornings.

If you're used to having a glass of fruit juice in the morning, remember that juices are very high in carbohydrates and are stripped of their beneficial fiber. (Orange juice, for example, has 25 carbohydrates in a single cup, and apple juice has 29.) Most of the breakfasts included here contain fruit, so you shouldn't need to have fruit juice. For those recipes that don't include fruit, such as the tofu scramble, go ahead and eat a piece of fruit along with your meal.

# Cereal with Fruit

*If you're like me, on most weekday mornings you won't have time to make a nutritious breakfast. But breakfast is one of the most important meals of the day and should never be skipped. The easiest breakfast is simply a bowl of high-fiber cereal with soymilk and a cup of fruit. Here are some good choices. The nutritional contents below are based on the recommended serving size (anywhere from ½ cup to 1 cup) on the cereal boxes.*

|  | Calories | Carbs | Fiber | Protein | Fat |
|---|---|---|---|---|---|
| Quaker Crunchy Corn Bran | 90 | 23 | 5 | 1 | 1 |
| All Bran | 78 | 22 | 10 | 4 | 1 |
| Bran Flakes | 96 | 24 | 5 | 3 | 1 |
| Fiber One | 59 | 24 | 14 | 2 | 1 |
| Post Bran Flakes | 100 | 24 | 5 | 3 | 1 |
| Special K | 117 | 22 | 1 | 7 | 1 |
| Wheat Chex | 104 | 24 | 3 | 3 | 1 |
| Wheaties | 110 | 24 | 3 | 3 | 1 |
| Whole Grain | 97 | 23 | 2 | 2 | 1 |
| Back to Nature High Protein | 140 | 25 | 3 | 12 | 1 |
| Kashi Go Lean Crunch | 190 | 36 | 8 | 9 | 3 |

Combine any of the above cereals, or other cereals with either a high fiber or high protein count (especially if you're following the Zone), and a low-carbohydrate count, with:

|  | Calories | Carbs | Fiber | Protein | Fat |
|---|---|---|---|---|---|
| ½ cup of vanilla soymilk | 75 | 11 | 0 | 3.5 | 2 |

and a serving of fruit such as:

|  | Calories | Carbs | Fiber | Protein |
|---|---|---|---|---|
| 1 apple | 72 | 19 | 3 | 0 |
| 1 cup blackberries | 62 | 14 | 8 | 2 |
| 1 cup blueberries | 83 | 21 | 3 | 1 |
| ¼ cantaloupe | 46 | 6 | 2 | 2 |
| 1 orange | 62 | 15 | 3 | 1 |
| 2 slices pineapple | 80 | 22 | 2 | 0 |
| 20 raspberries | 20 | 4 | 2 | 0 |

Each serving contains 1 serving of fruit, 1 serving of protein, and 1 serving of grain.

# Oatmeal with Raspberries

### Serves 2

*Whole oats are an excellent source of fiber. Do not use quick oats. They have had the outer hulls removed to allow for faster cooking time, resulting in a loss of fiber. Only old fashioned, steel cut oats contain significant amounts of fiber. Even with steel cut oats, the whole breakfast takes only five minutes to prepare, making it quick enough for the prework rush. Since the fiber content in the oats is so high, the net carbs drop to 45 grams per serving. If you are concerned about raising your protein to meet the Zone standard, you can add a half scoop (1½ tablespoons) of protein powder, which will add 12 more grams of protein.*

1¾ cups vanilla soymilk

1 cup old-fashioned oatmeal

Sprinkle of cinnamon

2 tablespoons chopped walnuts

2 cups raspberries

Pour the soymilk into a small saucepan, and bring to a boil. Stir in the oats. Cook the oats in the soymilk for about 5 minutes over medium heat, stirring occasionally.

Sprinkle cinnamon and walnuts on top, and serve with the raspberries

Each serving contains 2 servings of fruit, 1 serving of protein, and 1 serving of grain.

| | |
|---|---|
| Protein: 13 grams | 14% of calories |
| Fat: 12 grams | 29% of calories |
| Carbs: 53 grams | 57% of calories |
| Calories: 405 | Fiber: 8 grams |

# "Chorizo" and Soy Sausage Scramble

Serves 2

*My dad used to make chorizo and eggs when I was growing up, and it was one thing that I missed after going vegetarian. So I was thrilled to discover a meatless chorizo! The soy chorizo, which can be found in the deli case or freezer of some grocery stores, is very flavorful. Serve with fruit and whole grain toast.*

| | |
|---|---|
| 1 tablespoon olive oil | 8 ounces (½ pound) firm tofu, drained |
| ½ cup onion, diced | Salt and pepper to taste |
| 2 veggie sausage patties, chopped | |
| 2 ounces meatless chorizo | |

In a large nonstick saucepan, heat the oil over medium heat. Sauté the onions, sausage pieces, and "chorizo" for 2 minutes or until the onion turns translucent.

Crumble the drained tofu into the pan, and sauté the tofu with the other ingredients until all of the ingredients are mixed together and hot. Add salt and pepper to taste. The "chorizo" will be completely melted into the tofu by the time it's done.

---

Nutritional analysis uses Soyrizo Meatless Chorizo and Yves Veggie Sausage Patties. Each serving contains 2 servings of protein.
With fruit and toast, it contains 1 serving of fruit and 1 serving of fiber.

| | |
|---|---|
| Protein: 20 grams | 30% of calories |
| Fat: 17 grams | 59% of calories |
| Carbs: 7 grams | 11% of calories |
| Calories: 253 | Fiber: 2.5 grams |

# Tofu Scramble with Veggie Bacon

### Serves 2

*This is my favorite weekend breakfast. You can add any number of vegetables to this scramble, such as spinach, broccoli, asparagus, artichoke hearts, or zucchini. Serve with fruit, which will bring the carb count up to a Zone level.*

1 tablespoon olive oil

½ onion, diced

2 garlic cloves, minced

¼ bell pepper, chopped

⅛ teaspoon pepper

⅛ teaspoon paprika

⅛ teaspoon cumin

⅛ teaspoon chili powder

⅛ teaspoon red pepper

4 slices vegetarian bacon, sliced into strips

2 cups sliced mushrooms

8 ounces (½ pound) medium-firm tofu, drained

1 small tomato, chopped

In a large nonstick saucepan, heat 1 teaspoon of the oil over medium heat. Sauté the onions, garlic, bell pepper, and spices for 5 minutes or until the onion turns translucent. Remove from the pan and set aside.

Sauté the veggie bacon in the same pan for about 5 minutes, turning once, until browned and slightly crispy. Remove from the pan and set aside.

Sauté the mushrooms in the same pan in another teaspoon of the oil, until they are soft and any liquid has evaporated, about 5 minutes. Remove from the pan and set aside.

Crumble the drained tofu into the pan, add the remaining teaspoon of oil, and sauté until lightly browned. Add the onion mix back in, along with the mushrooms, bacon, and fresh tomato. Cook for another 5 minutes.

Nutritional analysis based on Yves Veggie Canadian Bacon.
Each serving contains 2 servings of vegetables and 2 servings of protein.
With a piece of fruit, add 1 serving of fruit.

| | |
|---|---|
| Protein: 20 grams, | 38% of calories |
| Fat: 11 grams | 46% of calories |
| Carbs: 9 grams | 16% of calories |
| Calories: 224 | Fiber: 3 grams |

# Strawberry Smoothie

Serves 2

*You can prepare large quantities of smoothies ahead of time and refrigerate in a closeable container until breakfast. Try different combinations of fruit to satisfy different taste buds. Add in a little protein powder to make this appropriate for the Zone, or a slice of bread to add fiber.*

12 ounces (¾ pound) silken tofu

⅔ banana

⅔ cup chopped frozen strawberries (about 6 small strawberries)

2 tablespoons frozen apple juice concentrate

Blend all of the ingredients in a food processor or blender until smooth. If using fresh instead of frozen strawberries, add two ice cubes to the mix.

Each serving contains 1 serving of fruit and 1 serving of protein.
Add a slice of whole grain toast for fiber.

| | |
|---|---|
| Protein: 11 grams | 25% of calories |
| Fat: 5 grams | 27% of calories |
| Carbs: 20 grams | 48% of calories |
| Calories: 163 | Fiber: 4 grams |

# *Berry Banana Smoothie*

Serves 2

*This is a very easy breakfast to make, and very yummy. It is also an excellent source of fiber. If you are not concerned about the extra protein needed for the Zone diet, omit the protein powder. For the Zone, keep the powder, and also add in your favorite nut butter for extra fat. After subtracting the fiber from the blackberries, the net carb count is only 40 grams*

2 cups low fat vanilla soy yogurt

1½ scoops (4½ tablespoons, about 42 g) vanilla soy protein powder
   (optional)

¼ teaspoon cinnamon

1 cup frozen blackberries

1 banana

Combine all of the ingredients in a food processor or blender, and process until smooth. If you're using fresh berries instead of frozen, add about 4 cubes of ice.

Each serving contains 2 servings of fruit, 1 serving of protein
(2 with protein powder).

| | |
|---|---|
| Protein: 28 grams | 32% of calories |
| Fat: 5 grams | 14% of calories |
| Carbs: 49 grams | 54% of calories |
| Calories: 366 | Fiber: 9.5 grams |

Without the protein powder, the ratios are as follows:

| | |
|---|---|
| Protein: 10.5 grams | 15% of calories |
| Fat: 5 grams | 15% of calories |
| Carbs: 49 grams | 70% of calories |
| Calories: 284 | Fiber: 9.5 grams |

# Four Berry Smoothie

### Serves 2

*If you like berries, this smoothie is for you. Serve with a slice of whole grain toast. Add protein powder if you want to bring the smoothie into the Zone.*

12 ounces (¾ pound) silken tofu

½ cup sliced frozen strawberries

½ cup frozen blueberries

½ cup frozen raspberries

¼ cup cranberry juice

¼ teaspoon vanilla extract

Blend all of the ingredients in a food processor or blender until smooth. If you are using fresh instead of frozen berries, add two ice cubes to the mix.

---

Each serving contains 2 servings of fruit and 1 serving of protein.
Add one slice of whole grain toast for 1 serving of grain.

| | |
|---|---|
| Protein: 10 grams | 25% of calories |
| Fat: 5 grams | 29% of calories |
| Carbs: 18 grams | 46% of calories |
| Calories: 157 | Fiber: 3.5 grams |

# Fruit Salad with Soy Yogurt

Serves 1

*This is as easy as picking your favorite fruits from the list below and topping with yogurt. If you're not concerned about getting more protein, you can omit the protein powder. To bring down the carb count, omit one of the categories of fruit.*

1 cup plain soy yogurt with ½ scoop (1½ tablespoons, 21 g) soy protein powder

*Choose two of the following fruits:*

10 raspberries

4 strawberries

5 grapes

⅛ cantaloupe

*Plus one of the following:*

1 apple, sliced

½ mango, sliced

½ papaya, sliced

*Plus one of the following:*

1 kiwi, sliced

⅛ honeydew melon

½ pear, sliced

1 slice pineapple

1 cup blackberries

½ banana, sliced

½ cup blueberries

Mix all of the fruit in a large bowl with the yogurt and protein powder.

| Each serving contains 3 servings of fruit and 1 serving of protein. | |
| --- | --- |
| Protein: 21 grams | 23% of calories |
| Fat: 4 grams | 10% of calories |
| Carbs: 61 grams | 67% of calories |
| Calories: 379 | Fiber: 3 grams |

# *Soups*

To me, there's nothing more comforting than curling up on the couch with dinner in my favorite "Talk Soup" bowl and a big spoon.

For many of us, soup comes in a can, and while easy to prepare, very few canned soups are nutritious, and almost none (especially vegetarian soups) are appropriate for a low-carb diet.

Yet soups that are made with fresh ingredients are good for you, yummy, easy to prepare, and even easier to consume.

The recipes in this chapter, like most in this book, are made to serve two people as a side dish or one as a main dish, but all can easily be made in larger quantities, resulting in perfect leftovers for lunch or dinner.

# Cream of Mushroom Soup

Serves 2 as a side dish

*If you grew up on Campbell's cream of mushroom soup, you'll know why I included this recipe. There's nothing like a creamy mushroom soup to make you feel warm and cozy. This nutritious version is good for Zone advocates but should be accompanied by a fiber-rich vegetable, such as broccoli or a salad, as a side dish.*

½ onion, chopped

2 garlic cloves, minced

1 tablespoon olive oil

2 cups sliced mushrooms

¼ teaspoon dried thyme

¼ teaspoon paprika

Salt and pepper to taste

⅓ cup sherry

8 ounces (½ pound) silken tofu

2 cups vegetable stock

½ teaspoon vegetarian
    Worcestershire sauce
    or soy sauce

In a large saucepan, sauté the onion and garlic in the oil until the onion is translucent. Add the mushrooms and spices, and sauté for 5 minutes. Add the sherry and simmer for 5 more minutes.

In a blender, combine the tofu and the vegetable stock (which should be cool) for at least 5 minutes until very smooth. Add the tofu mixture to the saucepan, and stir into the mushrooms. Add the Worcestershire sauce, stirring constantly, and simmer for another 2 minutes.

Each serving contains 2 servings of vegetable and ½ serving of protein.

| | |
|---|---|
| Protein: 10 grams | 33% of calories |
| Fat: 4 grams | 30% of calories |
| Carbs: 11 grams | 37% of calories |
| Calories: 121 | Fiber: 1 gram |

# Cream of Broccoli Soup

Serves 2 as a side dish; serves 1 as a main dish
(nutritional analysis is for single side serving)

*This is a very mellow soup, with very few spices or ingredients. But if you love broccoli like I do, it is the BEST. It also has a very good fiber content, thanks to the fabulous broccoli. Serve with a salad.*

**4 cups chopped fresh broccoli**
**2 cups vegetable stock**
**Salt and pepper to taste**
**4 ounces (¼ pound) silken tofu**

In a large saucepan, combine the broccoli and stock. Bring to a boil, reduce the heat, and simmer until the broccoli is tender, about 15 minutes. Add salt and pepper to taste, and set the soup aside to cool.

Puree the soup in a food processor or blender with the silken tofu until it is very smooth. Pour the soup back into the pot and reheat before serving.

Each serving contains 4 servings of vegetable and ⅓ serving of protein.

| | |
|---|---|
| Protein: 7.3 grams | 29% of calories |
| Fat: 1.6 grams | 15% of calories |
| Carbs: 14.3 grams | 56% of calories |
| Calories: 108 | Fiber: 4 grams |

# Tofu Miso Soup

Serves 2 as a side dish

*This delicate Japanese soup derives its flavor from miso, a fermented bean paste usually made from soybeans (easy to find in most natural food stores). You can experiment with different kinds of miso; I prefer the darker and red varieties (which are stronger in flavor and have been aged longer), but all are good. Serve with sushi or another protein/vegetable combination.*

2½ cups vegetable stock

4 ounces (¼ pound) firm tofu, sliced into ½-inch thick cubes

3 tablespoons miso paste

1 scallion, sliced

1 sheet nori (dehydrated seaweed), ripped into small pieces

Bring 2 cups of the stock to a boil in a medium saucepan. Add the tofu cubes and continue boiling.

Meanwhile, dissolve the miso paste in the remaining ½ cup of stock. Turn off the heat and add the miso mixture to the pot. Add the sliced scallions and nori, stir briefly until nori gets soft, and serve.

Each serving contains ⅓ serving of protein.

| | |
|---|---|
| Protein: 7 grams | 27% of calories |
| Fat: 3 grams | 28% of calories |
| Carbs: 11 grams | 45% of calories |
| Calories: 115 | Fiber: 0 grams |

# Cauliflower, Leek, and Spinach Cream Soup

Serves 2 as a large sidedish

*This creamy soup has a high fiber content and tastes great too. It's based on a leek and potato cream soup that I used to make, with cauliflower standing in for the potatoes. The fiber brings the net carb count down to 22 carbs. Serve with a salad.*

½ medium head cauliflower, broken into florets (about 2 cups)

2 cups leeks, white parts only, thoroughly washed and sliced (about 3 leeks)

1 clove garlic, crushed

3 cups vegetable stock

½ teaspoon paprika

¼ teaspoon cayenne

5 ounces frozen spinach, thawed

Salt and pepper to taste

6 ounces (⅜ pound) silken tofu

In a large saucepan, combine the cauliflower, leeks, garlic, and stock. Bring to a boil, reduce the heat, and simmer, uncovered, until the vegetables are tender, about 15 minutes. Add the spices and the spinach, and simmer for another 5 minutes. Set aside to cool.

Puree the soup with the tofu in a food processor or blender until very smooth. Reheat and serve.

Each serving contains 2 servings of vegetable and ½ serving of protein.

| | |
|---|---|
| Protein: 10 grams | 21% of calories |
| Fat: 2.5 grams | 12% of calories |
| Carbs: 33 grams | 68% of calories |
| Calories: 199 | Fiber: 10.5 grams |

# Spicy Black Bean Soup

Serves 2 as a main dish

*This soup comes from my parents and is super-spicy! If you are not a fan of very hot food, please feel free to reduce the amounts of spices and peppers in this soup. But if you have a cold or are feeling a little down, there's nothing like a really hot dish like this to pick you up. This may seem high in carbohydrates relative to the protein, but the beans contain so much fiber they reduce the net carbs to 38 grams.*

½ tablespoon olive oil

½ yellow onion, chopped

½ jalapeño pepper, seeded and chopped

2 cloves garlic, minced

One 15-ounce can black beans, rinsed and drained

1 cup vegetable stock

One 10-ounce can diced tomatoes

½ teaspoon ground cumin

½ teaspoon chili powder

½ teaspoon ground cayenne

¼ teaspoon crushed red peppers

1 cup plain soy yogurt

Chopped cilantro for garnish

In a large saucepan, heat the olive oil over medium heat. Add the onion, jalapeño, and garlic, and sauté, stirring occasionally, until the onions are softened.

Add the beans to the saucepan along with the vegetable stock, tomatoes, and spices. Mix everything well and bring to a boil.

Reduce the heat to low, cover the pot, and simmer, stirring occasionally, until the soup is well blended, about half an hour. Remove the soup from the heat, and set aside to cool.

Pour half the soup into a food processor or blender, and process until smooth. Pour the blended soup back into the saucepan with the unprocessed soup. Simmer over medium heat for another 5 minutes, until the soup is heated through.

Turn off the heat and stir in the soy yogurt. Serve each portion with a sprinkle of chopped cilantro.

| Each serving contains 1 serving of vegetables and 1 serving of protein. | |
| --- | --- |
| Protein: 13 grams | 18% of calories |
| Fat: 3.5 grams | 11% of calories |
| Carbs: 51 grams | 71% of calories |
| Calories: 278 | Fiber: 12 grams |

# Curried Cauliflower Dal Soup

Serves 2 as a main dish

*This is a rich and filling Indian dish. Do not use American lentils for this! Moong dal (mung beans), toor dal (yellow lentils), and masoor dal (red lentils) are all good choices. You can buy dal at any Indian grocery store or other store that carries ethnic or Asian food items.*

½ cup uncooked dal

1½ to 3 cups water or vegetable stock

½ large cauliflower

¼ cup chopped yellow onion

2 cloves garlic, minced

2 teaspoons minced peeled fresh ginger

½ tablespoon olive oil

1 tablespoon curry powder

¼ teaspoon chili powder

Salt and pepper to taste

½ cup tomato puree

Bring the dal and about 1½ cups water or stock to a boil, Remove the foam, reduce the heat to a simmer, and cook for about an hour, until the dal is soft and most of the water is gone. If your soup thickens up too much, feel free to add more water to achieve the consistency you prefer.

At the same time, boil or steam the cauliflower in a separate pot until it's soft, about 20 minutes. It will easily break apart once soft.

In a saucepan, sauté the onion, garlic, and ginger in the oil until the onion is translucent. Add the spices and cook for another minute.

Mash the cooked dal into the onion and spice mixture.

When the cauliflower is tender, pour the dal and onion mixture back into the cauliflower pot, along with at least 1 cup of the cooking water or stock. Stir to break up any remaining cauliflower pieces.

Stir in the tomato puree, and cook for another 15 minutes or so, until all of the ingredients are well blended.

| Each serving contains 1 serving of vegetable and 1 serving of protein. | |
| --- | --- |
| Protein: 13 grams | 19% of calories |
| Fat: 4 grams | 12% of calories |
| Carbs: 46 grams | 69% of calories |
| Calories: 231 | Fiber: 18 grams |

# White Bean Soup with Spinach, Mushrooms and Leeks

Serves 2 as a large side dish or main dish

*This soup is modified minestrone. You can use any mushroom you like in this dish, or a variety. I used brown crimini mushrooms mixed with shiitake. This is an excellent source of fiber, and with the fiber, the net carb count is actually down to 42.*

1 tablespoon olive oil

2 cups leeks, white parts only, thoroughly washed and sliced (about 3 leeks)

2 cloves garlic, crushed

3 cups sliced mushrooms

1 teaspoon cumin

1 teaspoon oregano

3 cups vegetable stock

One 15-ounce can white beans, rinsed and drained

5 ounces frozen spinach, thawed

Salt and pepper to taste

Heat the oil in a large stockpot over medium-high heat. Add the leeks, garlic and mushrooms, and sauté for 4 to 5 minutes, until all of the vegetables are soft. Add the spices and stir to blend.

Add the stock, white beans, and spinach, and bring the mixture to a boil. Simmer, uncovered, for about 20 minutes, letting the flavors mingle and the stock thicken somewhat. Season the soup to taste with salt and pepper.

| Each serving contains 3 servings of vegetables and 1 to 2 servings of protein. | |
| --- | --- |
| Protein: 18 grams | 19% of calories |
| Fat: 8 grams | 19% of calories |
| Carbs: 60 grams | 62% of calories |
| Calories: 335 | Fiber: 18 grams |

# Cream of Tomato Soup

Serves 2 as a main dish; 4 as a side dish;
nutritional analysis assumes 2 main dish servings

*This is a very soothing soup and is perfect for a hot lunch on a cold winter day. To increase the protein content, serve with a simple protein item like a tofu dog.*

1½ tablespoons olive oil

1 clove garlic, minced

½ cup chopped onion

2 pounds tomatoes (about 4 large tomatoes)

2 cups vegetable stock

1 packet Splenda (optional)

6 ounces (¾ pound) silken tofu

Salt and pepper to taste

6 large fresh basil leaves, chopped

Heat the olive oil in a large stockpot over medium-high heat. Add the garlic and onion, and sauté for 4 to 5 minutes, until the onion is soft and transparent. Stir in the tomatoes, the stock, and the Splenda, if using, and bring to a boil. Reduce the heat and simmer, uncovered, for 15 minutes. Set aside to cool.

Puree the cooled soup in batches in a food processor or blender with the tofu until very well blended. Add salt and pepper to taste, and stir in the basil. Reheat and serve immediately.

Each serving contains 2 servings of vegetables and ½ serving of protein.

| | |
|---|---|
| Protein: 8 grams | 14% of calories |
| Fat: 13 grams | 51% of calories |
| Carbs: 20 grams | 35% of calories |
| Calories: 213 | Fiber: 3 grams |

# Lentils with Mushrooms

Makes 2 main dish servings

*This is an old family recipe and makes a very hearty meal. The mango hot sauce adds extra zest. While it looks like it has a high carbohydrate count, the net carb count is actually only 49 grams, thanks to the fiber in the lentils.*

3 cups vegetable stock

1 cup dried lentils

¼ cup chopped onion

2 cups sliced mushrooms

2 tablespoons olive oil

1 stalk celery, chopped

½ teaspoon dried oregano

Salt and pepper to taste

1 cup tomato puree

½ teaspoon mango habanero hot
    sauce (optional; you can also use
    a generic hot pepper sauce)

1 tablespoon vinegar

In a large saucepan, bring the vegetable stock to boil, and add the dried lentils. Reduce the heat and simmer for 1 hour. In another pan, sauté the onion and mushrooms in the oil until soft, and set aside.

After the lentils have cooked for an hour, combine all the ingredients, except the hot sauce and vinegar, and continue cooking for at least another hour, until the lentils are tender and the flavors are well mixed. You may need to add more stock (or water) while the lentils are cooking if they get too thick. Add the hot sauce and vinegar, and serve.

Each serving contains 3 servings of vegetables and 1 to 2 servings of protein.

| | |
|---|---|
| Protein: 25 grams | 19% of calories |
| Fat: 14 grams | 25% of calories |
| Carbs: 72 grams | 56% of calories |
| Calories: 443 | Fiber: 23 grams |

# Chilled Avocado Tomatillo Soup

### Serves 2

*This soup is served chilled, like gazpacho, so remember to make this well
ahead of time! It has a very high fat content (although the fat comes primarily
from nutritious avocados), so it should be enjoyed as an occasional treat. Serve
with a simple protein item like tofu hotdogs.*

½ pound tomatillos, husked
and rinsed

2 garlic cloves, peeled

½ jalapeño chili, stemmed
and seeded

½ tablespoon olive oil

½ tablespoon lime juice

1½ ripe avocados, seeded and
peeled

1 cup vegetable stock

Salt to taste

½ cup plain soy yogurt

Place the tomatillos, garlic, and chili on a baking sheet. Drizzle with the oil
and toss until evenly coated. Roast in a preheated 450°F oven until nicely
browned and soft, about 20 minutes. Set aside to cool.

Place the roasted vegetables (with any of the juices that remain in the pan
from roasting), the lime juice, avocado, and stock into a food processor or
blender, and puree until smooth. Stir in salt to taste, and the soy yogurt.
Refrigerate until well chilled, at least two hours.

Each serving contains 2 servings of vegetables and ½ serving of protein.

| | |
|---|---|
| Protein: 5.5 grams | 6% of calories |
| Fat: 26.5 grams | 68% of calories |
| Carbs: 23 grams | 26% of calories |
| Calories: 318 | Fiber: 11 grams |

# Red Pepper Soup with Basil Cream

Serves 2

*This light soup is served chilled, like gazpacho, so remember to make this well ahead of time! Serve with a protein-rich salad or main dish.*

2 large red bell peppers
½ cup chopped yellow onions
1 tablespoon olive oil
½ teaspoon paprika
2 cups vegetable stock
Salt and pepper to taste
4 ounces (¼ pound) silken tofu
¼ cup soy sour cream
4 large basil leaves

Broil the bell peppers, turning occasionally until all sides are black, bubbly, and crispy. Place the broiled peppers into a small paper bag, and close. Set aside to for the peppers to steam.

In about 20 minutes, remove the peppers and carefully peel off the skins. Slice open and remove the seeds and core. Cut the skinned and seeded peppers into ½-inch wide strips.

In a large saucepan, sauté the onion in the oil until translucent. Add the pepper slices and paprika, and cook for another minute.

Add the stock, salt, and pepper to the pot, and bring to a boil. Cover, reduce the heat, and simmer for about 15 minutes. Set aside to cool.

Puree the cooled soup and tofu in a food processor or blender until very smooth. Transfer the soup to a sealed container and refrigerate for four hours, or until well chilled.

When ready to serve, blend the sour cream with the basil leaves in a food processor or blender, creating a creamy green sauce. Serve the soup in bowls and swirl some of the basil cream on top.

Nutritional analysis based on Tofutti Sour Supreme sour cream.
Each serving contains 1 serving of vegetables and ½ serving of protein.

| | |
|---|---|
| Protein: 5 grams | 15% of calories |
| Fat: 7 grams | 42% of calories |
| Carbs: 15 grams | 43% of calories |
| Calories: 139 | Fiber: 0 grams |

# Dixie's Butternut Squash Soup

Serves 2 as a main dish

*This soup comes from my mom's aunt Dixie and is a big hit at my family's home. If you think you don't like squash, you should try this recipe anyway. It is so amazingly rich and creamy, it will make you rethink your squash aversion.*

½ onion, minced

2 cups peeled and cubed butternut squash

2 cups vegetable stock

2 tablespoons nonhydrogenated margarine

2 tablespoons soy flour

2 cups plain soymilk

I teaspoon curry powder (or more to taste)

½ teaspoon cayenne (optional)

Salt and pepper to taste

½ cup plain soy yogurt

In a large covered saucepan, cook the onions and squash in the stock until they are very soft. Remove from the heat to cool. Process the squash mixture in a food processor or blender until smooth. Set aside.

Make a roux by melting the margarine in the same saucepan the onions and squash were cooked in. Stir in the flour and simmer the margarine/flour mixture for about 1 minute while stirring constantly. Remove the roux from heat. Whisk in the soymilk, followed by the pureed squash. Add the spices. Return the soup to the stove, and reheat until hot and creamy.

Serve in shallow bowls, swirling a little chili puree (optional; see recipe below) over each serving and adding a dollop of soy yogurt to top.

# Chili Puree

*Be careful when handling chilies. Never use your fingernails to try to split or seed a chili, and always wash your hands well after handling them to avoid getting anything into your eyes or other sensitive areas.*

2 dried New Mexico or California chilies, about 4 inches long
¾ cup water
1 tablespoon chopped onions
¼ teaspoon powdered cinnamon

Rinse the chilies, break off and discard the stems, and shake out as many seeds as you can. With a pair of scissors, cut the chilies into ½-inch pieces and drop into a medium saucepan.

Add the water, onions, and cinnamon. Bring to a boil over high heat, then reduce the heat, cover, and simmer until the chilies are soft, about 5 to 10 minutes.

In a blender or food processor, puree the mixture until smooth. Press the mixture through a strainer set over a bowl. Stir in salt and pepper to taste.

| Each serving of soup contains 2 servings of vegetables and 1 serving of protein. | |
| --- | --- |
| Protein: 10 grams | 11% of calories |
| Fat: 16 grams | 40% of calories |
| Carbs: 43 grams | 49% of calories |
| Calories: 353 | Fiber: 0 grams |

# Hot and Sour Soup

### Serves 2

*This recipe comes from my sister-in-law and is best made with wood ear mushrooms, but any kind of Chinese mushroom can be used. Serve with steamed Chinese greens like gai lon, bok choy, or Chinese broccoli, with a bit of soy sauce on top.*

1½ tablespoons soy sauce

1½ tablespoons vinegar

¼ teaspoon white pepper

1 tablespoon sesame oil

¼ teaspoon hot pepper sauce

3 cups vegetable stock

2 ounces Chinese mushrooms, washed and sliced (about 1 cup)

¼ cup bamboo shoots

1½ tablespoons cornstarch

3 tablespoons water

6 ounces (⅜ pound) firm tofu, drained and cut into ¾-inch cubes

1 scallion, sliced

In a small bowl, mix the soy sauce, vinegar, pepper, sesame oil and hot pepper sauce. Set aside.

In a medium saucepan, combine the vegetable stock, mushrooms, and bamboo shoots. Bring to a boil and simmer over medium heat for about 5 minutes. Stir in more soy sauce or hot sauce to taste.

Mix the cornstarch and water, and add to the stock. Stir for a couple of minutes to blend and thicken. Add the tofu and continue to stir until all the flavors are blended, about 3 minutes.

Serve hot with a sprinkle of the scallions on top.

| Each serving contains 1 serving of vegetables and 1 serving of protein. | |
| --- | --- |
| Protein: 14 grams | 23% of calories |
| Fat: 11 grams | 40% of calories |
| Carbs: 23 grams | 38% of calories |
| Calories: 241 | Fiber: 5.5 grams |

# Soup with Chinese Greens and Tofu

Serves 2

*This is a light soup with a lot of flavor. Serve with Asparagus and Seitan Stir Fry, pages 122-23.*

½ tablespoon sesame oil

1 garlic clove, minced

1 tablespoon minced peeled fresh ginger

3 cups vegetable stock

1 cup chopped bok choy leaves

1 cup finely chopped Napa cabbage

2 tablespoons soy sauce

1 teaspoon rice vinegar

¼ teaspoon pepper

¼ cup bamboo shoots

4 ounces (¼ pound) firm tofu, drained and cut into ¾-inch cubes

1 scallion, sliced

½ cup snow peas, ends trimmed

Heat the oil in a medium saucepan, and sauté the garlic and ginger until fragrant, about 1 minute. Add the vegetable stock, greens, soy sauce, vinegar, pepper, and bamboo shoots. Bring to a boil and simmer for 5 minutes.

Add the tofu, scallions, and snow peas, and simmer for another 10 minutes.

| Each serving contains 1 serving of vegetables and ½ serving of protein. | |
| --- | --- |
| Protein: 9 grams | 26% of calories |
| Fat: 6 grams | 38% of calories |
| Carbs: 12 grams | 35% of calories |
| Calories: 137 | Fiber: 4 grams |

# Salads

Salads are the stereotypical food for vegetarians, and for good reason. Made with fresh vegetables, salads are the ultimate health food and can be eaten as a side dish or a meal-in-one.

Salads are also fun to make—almost any vegetable, and many fruits and nuts as well, can be added to a basic salad, allowing for an almost infinite choice of meals. This chapter includes a recipe for a basic salad with lots of choices of ingredients, and a menu of dressings to mix and match. Additionally, you'll find a number of specialty salads based on the cuisines of cultures around the world.

For low-carb dieters who are vegetarian, salads rarely include enough protein to serve as stand-alone meals. Some of the salads in this chapter should indeed only be used as side dishes, as they have little or no protein in them (these are noted), but many can be complete meals, as they include enough soy protein to fulfill Zone or South Beach criteria.

# Oriental Cabbage Salad

### Serves 2

*If you like crunchy cabbage blended with a creamy dressing, this salad is for you. Serve with miso soup or a whole grain sandwich for a filling meal.*

2 tablespoons sesame oil

2 tablespoons rice wine vinegar

1 tablespoon soy sauce

2 teaspoons soy mayonnaise

4 ounces (¼ pound) silken tofu

4 cups finely chopped cabbage

2 scallions, chopped

2 tablespoons chopped cilantro leaves

1 tablespoon toasted sesame seeds

Prepare a dressing by blending the oil, vinegar, soy sauce, soy mayonnaise, and tofu in a food processor or blender until smooth.

Combine the dressing with the cabbage, scallions, and cilantro in a serving bowl. Sprinkle with the sesame seeds when ready to serve.

Nutritional analysis uses Nayonaise brand soy mayonnaise.
Each serving contains 2 servings of vegetables and ½ serving of protein.

| | |
|---|---|
| Protein: 8 grams | 13% of calories |
| Fat: 20 grams | 70% of calories |
| Carbs: 11 grams | 17% of calories |
| Calories: 195 | Fiber: 4 grams |

# Edamame Salad

Serves 2

*Edamame is a variety of green soybean that is often steamed and eaten right out of the pod. It's a tasty snack, as well as a basis for a simple salad. I prepare edamame the way I make lima beans: with oil, vinegar, salt, pepper, and garlic powder. It's very simple but very tasty. Serve with an Asian soup such as Soup with Chinese Greens and Tofu, page 70.*

16 ounces (1 pound) frozen edamame
   (makes about 1½ cups shelled beans)
1 tablespoon olive oil
2 tablespoons vinegar
Salt, pepper, and garlic powder to taste

Cook the edamame according to package instructions (boil for 4 to 5 minutes in salted water). Drain, rinse, and set aside to cool.

When cooled, shell the soybeans, discarding the pods.

Toss the beans together with the oil, vinegar, and spices, and serve warm or at room temperature.

---

Each serving contains 1 serving of protein.

| | |
|---|---|
| Protein: 12 grams | 23% of calories |
| Fat: 11.5 grams | 50% of calories |
| Carbs: 14 grams | 26% of calories |
| Calories: 210 | Fiber: 6 grams |

# Taco Salad

*We eat this easy dish about once a week as a stand-alone meal. The salsa is also excellent on fajitas, with Tofu Scramble, on a tofu burger, or by itself as a spicy salad. Other ingredients you can add if you are so inclined are minced cabbage, sliced radish, tomatillos, bell peppers, jicama, or whatever suits your fancy. We make our salsa the day before we plan to eat it so the flavors can really blend, but feel free to make and eat it the same day.*

*Taco "meat:"*
1⅓ cups soy hamburger crumbles
¼ teaspoon cumin
¼ teaspoon cayenne
¼ teaspoon chili powder
¼ teaspoon black pepper
¼ cup tomato sauce

*Salsa:*

2 medium tomatoes
½ medium red onion
1 serrano chili
1½ cups cilantro leaves
1 to 2 cloves garlic

4 teaspoons chopped scallion
½ teaspoon salt
½ teaspoon pepper
1 tablespoon vinegar
½ tablespoon lemon juice

4 cups chopped lettuce
½ avocado, chopped

To make the taco "meat," mix the burger crumbles in a medium saucepan with the spices and tomato sauce, and heat until the mixture is hot. This does not have to boil, as the crumbles are already cooked.

To make the salsa, use a very sharp knife or a vegetable chopper to chop the tomatoes, onion, chili, cilantro, garlic, and scallions into very small (1/16- to 1/8-inch) pieces. Using a food processor or blender will probably turn the tomatoes into mush, so you'll want to do this by hand. Transfer the salsa to a bowl, and stir in the salt, pepper, vinegar, and lemon juice.

To serve, place the taco mix into two big bowls, topped by two cups of chopped lettuce each, as well as a cup of salsa and half the avocado.

---

Nutritional analysis uses Morningstar Farms hamburger crumbles.
Each serving contains 3 servings of vegetables and 1 serving of protein.

| | |
|---|---|
| Protein: 13.5 grams | 19% of calories |
| Fat: 17.5 grams | 54% of calories |
| Carbs: 20 grams | 27% of calories |
| Calories: 260 | Fiber: 9 grams |

# Thai Cucumber Salad

Serves 2

*This is an unusual salad in that there's no oil and very little dressing. But the combination of sweet, spicy, and crunchy is very refreshing.*

1 cucumber

1 teaspoon salt

3 tablespoons rice vinegar

3 tablespoons water

2 packets Splenda or other artificial
   sweetener

½ small chili (such as serrano),
   seeded and minced

2 teaspoons minced red onion

2 teaspoons minced roasted, salted
   peanuts

Peel the cucumber and slice in half lengthwise, then seed and slice ¼-inch thick. Toss the cucumber slices and salt in a colander placed in the sink, and cover with enough ice cubes to completely cover the cucumber slices. Let sit in the sink to drain for about an hour.

To make a dressing, combine the vinegar, water, and Splenda in a small saucepan. Bring to a boil and simmer until the mixture becomes slightly syrupy and reduces to about ⅓ the amount, about 5 to 10 minutes. Pour the dressing into the bowl you plan to serve the salad in, and set aside to cool. This should take just a few minutes, as there won't be very much dressing. Just before you are ready to serve, stir the chili, onion, and peanuts into the dressing.

Rinse the cucumber slices with cold water, discarding the ice cubes. Toss the cucumbers with the dressing and serve.

| Each serving contains 1 serving of vegetables. | |
| --- | --- |
| Protein: 0.7 grams | 9% of calories |
| Fat: 1.5 grams | 43% of calories |
| Carbs: 4 grams | 48% of calories |
| Calories: 33 | Fiber: 0 grams |

# Japanese Salad

Makes 1 cup of dressing.
Use one tablespoon of dressing for every cup of vegetables.
Serving size assumes 2 cups of vegetables and 2 tablespoons dressing.

*I make this salad with crunchy iceberg lettuce and cabbage; there's something about the crunch of the vegetables mixed with the creamy sauce that's very appealing. Serve with a protein-rich dish like tofu miso soup or sushi.*

*Dressing:*

1 garlic clove

¼ medium onion

1 tablespoon chopped peeled fresh
   ginger

¼ teaspoon ground mustard powder

1 teaspoon tamari or other good
   quality soy sauce

1 teaspoon sesame oil

½ cup canola oil

¼ cup rice vinegar

2 tablespoons vinegar

Salt and pepper to taste

*Salad:*

1 cup chopped iceberg lettuce per
   person

1 cup finely chopped cabbage per
   person

In a food processor or blender, puree the garlic, onion, and ginger until smooth. Add the rest of the dressing ingredients, except the salt and pepper, and process until smooth and creamy. Add salt and pepper to taste. Toss with the chopped lettuce and cabbage.

| Each serving contains 2 servings of vegetables. | |
| --- | --- |
| Protein: 2 grams | 4% of calories |
| Fat: 8 grams | 15% of calories |
| Carbs: 20 grams | 82% of calories |
| Calories: 195 | Fiber: 4 grams |

# Tofu Coleslaw

Makes about 1 cup of dressing.

Use 1½ tablespoons of dressing for each cup of cabbage.

Serving size assumes 2 cups of cabbage and 3 tablespoons of dressing.

*This coleslaw tastes just like the picnic favorite, but is more nutritious. Serve with barbecued tofu dogs or Wieners and Beans, page 111, to make a classic American summer meal.*

4 ounces (¼ pound) silken tofu

¼ cup soy mayonnaise

1 teaspoon celery salt

1 teaspoon cider vinegar

1 teaspoon lemon juice

1 packet Splenda (optional)

1 teaspoon minced red onion

Black pepper to taste

*Per serving:*

1⅓ cups very finely chopped green cabbage

⅔ cup very finely chopped red cabbage (for color)

Blend the tofu, soy mayonnaise, celery salt, vinegar, lemon juice, Splenda (if using), and onion in the food processor or blender until very smooth. Stir in black pepper to taste. Mix the dressing with the cabbage, and serve.

Nutritional analysis uses Veganaise brand soy mayonnaise.
Each serving contains 1 serving of vegetables.

| | |
|---|---|
| Protein: 2.6 grams | 10% of calories |
| Fat: 7 grams | 58% of calories |
| Carbs: 8 grams | 32% of calories |
| Calories: 106 | Fiber: 4 grams |

# "Chicken" Caesar Salad

Makes ½ cup dressing.
Serving size assumes 2 cups lettuce mixed with 1 tablespoon dressing.

*This is a great vegetarian Caesar salad. You can use any vegetarian chicken substitute in this salad as long as you don't use a breaded cutlet.*

*Dressing:*

2 tablespoons lemon juice

1 teaspoon vegetarian
  Worcestershire sauce

¼ teaspoon salt

2 garlic cloves, minced

1 teaspoon wine vinegar

1 teaspoon fresh black pepper
  (freshly ground is best)

⅓ cup olive oil

1 tablespoon Dijon mustard

1 ounce (1/16 pound) silken tofu

2 soy chicken patties (approximately 2½ ounces each), sliced

4 cups bite-size pieces Romaine lettuce

In a food processor or blender, whip the dressing ingredients until smooth.

In a nonstick pan, warm the "chicken" patty slices, using little or no oil.

Toss the dressing with the lettuce, or refrigerate the dressing until ready to eat. Top the dressed lettuce with slices of "chicken." Top with more freshly ground pepper if you like your Caesar salad extra peppery.

---

Nutritional analysis uses Gardenburger "Flame Grilled Chik'n Grill" patties.
Each serving contains 2 servings of vegetables and 1 serving of protein.

| | |
|---|---|
| Protein: 13 grams | 28% of calories |
| Fat: 11 grams | 55% of calories |
| Carbs: 8 grams | 17% of calories |
| Calories: 185 | Fiber: 3 grams |

# Basic Vegetable Salad

*Salads make quick meals or side dishes that can increase your daily vegetable servings in an instant. Always have on hand your favorite salad ingredients and at least a couple of your favorite salad dressings, so you can make a salad in a moment's notice. None of these combinations contain enough protein to be a stand-alone meal, so they should be combined with a relatively low-fat main dish.*

Following is a basic guideline for a meal-size portion of salad for two people. Pick ingredients from the lettuce, vegetable, and bean categories, and select the salad dresssing of your choice. The nutritional analysis on the next page assumes approximately 2 tablespoons of oil or fat per serving (or half of each recipe's worth of dressing).

*Lettuce choices (4 heaping cups):*
Romaine, butter crunch, red or
    green leaf
Arugula
Spinach
Dandelion greens
Escarole
Radicchio
Other salad greens of your choice

*Bean choices (1 cup cooked):*
Kidney
Garbanzo
Other beans of your choice

*Vegetable choices (2 cups):*
Red onion slices
Tomato wedges or cherry tomatoes
Artichoke hearts
Broccoli florets
Celery slices
Cucumber slices, peeled
Bell pepper slices (red, green, or
    yellow)
Pepperoncini
Mushrooms, sliced

The following analysis is for the Basic Vegetable Salad
plus one of the salad dressings on pages 81 through 84.
Each serving of salad contains 4 servings of vegetables and 1 serving of protein.
(Double the amount of beans to increase the protein content.)
The dressing recipes using soy mayonnaise were analyzed
using Veganaise brand soy mayonnaise.

| | |
|---|---|
| Protein: 9 gram | 9% of calories |
| Fat: 29 grams | 64% of calories |
| Carbs: 28 grams | 27% of calories |
| Calories: 390 | Fiber: 6 grams |

# Basic Oil and Vinegar Dressing

Serves 2

4 tablespoons olive oil

1 tablespoon red wine vinegar

½ tablespoon lemon juice

1 garlic clove, crushed

Salt and pepper to taste

Pour all the ingredients into a small container. Close and shake to blend. Serve the dressing over salad (greens, vegetables, and beans) for two.

# Vinaigrette

Serves 2

4 tablespoons olive oil

1½ tablespoons red wine vinegar

½ teaspoon dried thyme

½ teaspoon dried dill

½ tablespoon fresh chives, minced

Salt and pepper to taste

Pour all the ingredients into a small container. Close and shake to blend. Serve the dressing over salad (greens, vegetables, and beans) for two.

# Creamy Cucumber Dill Dressing

Serves 2

1 tablespoon soy mayonnaise

4 tablespoons olive oil

1½ tablespoons lemon juice

2 tablespoons grated peeled and seeded cucumber

2 tablespoons fresh dill, or 2 teaspoons dried dill

1 garlic clove, crushed

¼ teaspoon mustard powder

Salt to taste

Pour all the ingredients into a small container. Close and shake to blend. Serve the dressing over salad (greens, vegetables, and beans) for two.

# Thousand Island Dressing

Serves 2

¼ cup soy mayonnaise

2 tablespoons ketchup

2 teaspoons lemon juice

2 tablespoons hamburger pickle relish

Pour all the ingredients into a small container. Close and shake to blend. Serve the dressing over salad (greens, vegetables, and beans) for two.

# Green Goddess Dressing

Serves 2

½ avocado, mashed

1 tablespoon mayonnaise

1 tablespoon olive oil

1 teaspoon lemon juice

2 tablespoons grated peeled and seeded cucumber

1 tablespoon chopped fresh dill, or 1 teaspoon dried dill

1 tablespoon chopped fresh parsley, or 1 teaspoon dried parsley

Salt to taste

Pour all the ingredients into a small container. Close and shake to blend. Serve the dressing over salad (greens, vegetables, and beans) for two.

# French Dressing

Serves 2

4 tablespoons olive oil

1½ tablespoons lemon juice

½ teaspoon Dijon mustard

1½ tablespoons lemon juice

1 garlic clove, crushed

Salt and pepper to taste

Pour all the ingredients into a small container. Close and shake to blend. Serve the dressing over salad (greens, vegetables, and beans) for two.

# Antipasto for Two

Serves 2

*My husband loves anything that comes pickled or marinated. This is a very easy salad, made with ingredients available at any grocery store. It's also perfect as a simple meal for the Zone.*

¼ cantaloupe, sliced

2 slices veggie bologna

2 slices veggie salami

2 ounces veggie pepperoni

¼ cup pepperoncini

½ cup sliced marinated mushrooms

4 marinated sweet cherry peppers

8 kalamata or nicoise olives (about ¼ cup)

½ cup marinated artichoke hearts

Arrange all the items on a serving platter.

---

Nutritional analysis uses Yves Veggie Bologna and Salami slices, and Vegi-Deli brand pepperoni.
Each serving contains 1 serving of vegetables,
1 serving of fruit, and 2 servings of protein.

| | |
|---|---|
| Protein: 20 grams | 31% of calories |
| Fat: 11 grams | 39% of calories |
| Carbs: 20 grams | 30% of calories |
| Calories: 225 | Fiber: 1.5 grams |

# Crunchy Seitan Salad with Spicy Sesame Dressing

Serves 2

*If you've been a vegetarian for a long time, eating a salad with veggie meat may seem strange to you. But this salad is really good with marinated and sautéed seitan on top.*

## Dressing:

2 tablespoons seasoned rice vinegar

1 teaspoon Dijon mustard

2 tablespoons vegetable oil

2 tablespoons sesame oil

½ teaspoon soy sauce

¼ cup chopped scallions

½ teaspoon dried crushed red pepper

Salt and pepper to taste

## Salad:

3 cups sliced napa cabbage

½ cucumber, sliced diagonally

½ cup chopped fresh mint

4 ounces (¼ pound) seitan, shredded

½ cup sliced, stemmed fresh shiitake mushrooms

2 teaspoons black sesame seeds (optional)

For the dressing, whisk the vinegar, mustard, oils, and soy sauce together in a medium bowl. Mix in the scallions and crushed red pepper. Season to taste with salt and pepper.

For the salad, combine the cabbage, cucumbers, and mint in a large bowl.

Heat a small wok or pan, and place the seitan pieces and sliced mushrooms in the wok, along with enough of the dressing to lightly cover. Cook over very high heat until the seitan and mushrooms are heated through and the seitan is slightly browned.

Toss the dressing, seitan, and mushrooms with the salad vegetables until well blended. Sprinkle with the sesame seeds. Serve immediately, or let cool and serve at room temperature.

Each serving contains 2 servings of vegetables and 1 to 2 servings of protein.

| | |
|---|---|
| Protein: 22.5 grams | 23% of calories |
| Fat: 29 grams | 65% of calories |
| Carbs: 13 grams | 13% of calories |
| Calories: 378 | Fiber: 3.6 grams |

# *"Potato" Salad*

### Serves 2

*This tastes surprisingly like the original and, like many low-carb dishes, substitutes cauliflower for potatoes. Serve with tofu dogs or Wieners and Beans, page 111.*

¼ head of cauliflower, cut into
    1-inch chunks (about 1 cup)

½ cup diced celery

4 ounces (¼ pound) firm tofu,
    drained

¼ cup diced red onion

⅓ cup soy mayonnaise

1 tablespoon red wine vinegar

½ teaspoon salt

¼ teaspoon pepper

1 packet Splenda (optional)

2 tablespoons chopped fresh parsley

Steam the cauliflower until just tender, but not soft. Drain. Mix the drained cauliflower chunks with the celery, tofu, and onions in a large bowl.

In a separate small bowl, mix the soy mayonnaise, vinegar, salt, pepper, and Splenda, if using. Pour the mixture over the vegetables, and stir well. Add the chopped parsley, stir once more, and refrigerate for at least an hour before serving.

---

Nutritional analysis uses Veganaise brand soy mayonnaise.
Each serving contains 1 serving of vegetables and ½ serving of protein.

| | |
|---|---|
| Protein: 6.5 grams | 9% of calories |
| Fat: 25 grams | 78% of calories |
| Carbs: 9 grams | 12% of calories |
| Calories: 293 | Fiber: 4 grams |

# Sandwiches and Lunch

Lunch, like breakfast, is a critical meal for dieters in particular. Skipping lunch is the quickest route to afternoon snacking or evening overeating, sabotaging a day's good intentions.

Likewise, not making and bringing a nutritious lunch to work or to school means that you will be tempted by the dining choices near your work place—and often the choices of your work or school mates as well. If lunch time arrives and you are not prepared with a yummy, good-for-you meal, it will be all too easy for you to pick something up at a fast food restaurant or cafeteria and almost impossible to stay on your diet.

But by planning your lunch the night before and making meals that not only include a balance of good carbs, protein, and fiber, but are satisfying and enjoyable, you set yourself up for success.

Remember to also make extras of many of the soups or main dishes in this book, so that you can easily bring leftovers for lunch.

# Oriental Mock Chicken Salad in Pita Bread

Serves 2

*The "chicken salad" can be prepared in larger quantities in advance, so that you can have salads or sandwiches a few times from one large batch. If you are on Phase One of the South Beach diet, omit the pita bread and eat the salad on a bed of lettuce. This meal is very close to Zone proportions.*

12 ounces (¾ pound) soft tofu, diced

2 tablespoons soy mayonnaise

2 scallions, chopped

2 tablespoons diced celery

½ teaspoon lemon juice

2 tablespoons chopped cilantro leaves

1 teaspoon grated peeled fresh ginger

½ teaspoon curry powder

Salt and pepper to taste

1 whole wheat pita bread

Shredded lettuce

Mix the tofu, soy mayonnaise, scallions, celery, lemon juice, cilantro, ginger, and spices in a bowl. Serve the salad in the whole wheat pita with lettuce.

Nutritional analysis uses Nayonaise brand soy mayonnaise.
Each serving contains ½ serving of vegetables,
1 to 2 servings of protein, and 2 servings of grain.

| | |
|---|---|
| Protein: 19 grams | 25% of calories |
| Fat: 12 grams | 36% of calories |
| Carbs: 30 grams | 39% of calories |
| Calories: 303 | Fiber: 4 grams |

# Cold Cut Sandwiches

Serves 1

*Unlike Mom's sandwiches, full of meat, white bread, and iceberg lettuce, these sandwiches are easy, good for you, and yummy too. Good breads include anything that says "sprouted," "multi-grain," "7-grain," or includes lots of soy protein. Look for breads with from 70 to 100 calories per slice, 10 to 19 grams carbohydrates, 4 to 6 grams protein, and at least 2 grams fiber per slice.*

2 slices of whole grain bread

1 teaspoon soy mayonnaise

1 teaspoon Dijon mustard

2 slices tomato

1 slice red or white onion

1 leaf of red lettuce

Handful of sliced pepperoncini

½ pickle, sliced

4 slices vegetarian salami, turkey, or bologna

*Other good additions:*

2 slices bell pepper

Marinated jalapeño pepper rings

¼ avocado, sliced (which would bring the fat content to a Zone level)

Artichoke hearts

Sliced mushrooms

Spinach

Sliced olives

Spread each slice of bread with the soy mayonnaise and the mustard. In the order of your choosing, assemble the other ingredients, sandwich-style. Eat up!

---

Nutritional analysis uses Yves Veggie bologna and salami and Veganaise brand soy mayonnaise.

Each serving contains ½ serving of vegetables, 2 servings of protein, and 2 servings of grain.

| | |
|---|---|
| Protein: 25 grams | 44% of calories |
| Fat: 2 grams | 7% of calories |
| Carbs: 29 grams | 50% of calories |
| Calories: 265 | Fiber: 5 grams |

# Tofu Falafel with Hummus

Makes 16 falafel patties and 2 cups of hummus

Approximately 4 servings

*I am a huge fan of falafel. After starting on a low-carb diet, I was disappointed to find that falafel is high in carbohydrates, due mostly to the white flour and breadcrumbs. This version has tofu to increase the protein and skips the flour and breadcrumbs altogether. Thanks to the garbanzo beans and spices, this version is just as good as the original. You might want to make the falafel mix the day before, as the flavors will blend overnight.*

*Falafel:*

4 ounces (¼ pound) firm tofu, drained

1 cup cooked garbanzo beans (chickpeas), rinsed and drained

2 garlic cloves

4 tablespoons chopped parsley

1 teaspoon cumin

1 teaspoon coriander

Salt and pepper to taste

1 small white onion

½ cup soy flour

3 tablespoons oil

*Hummus:*

1½ cups cooked garbanzo beans (chickpeas), rinsed and drained

2 garlic cloves

¼ to ½ cup tahini

⅓ cup lemon juice

Salt to taste

½ cup water if necessary to thin hummus


Whole wheat pita bread (optional, one per person)

Lettuce, tomato, and red onions for garnish

For the falafel, put all of the ingredients together into a food processor or blender, except the oil. Blend until smooth. Form the falafel paste into 16 patties, and fry in the oil. (Alternatively, you can bake the patties on an oiled or non-stick baking pan in a preheated 350°F oven for 20 minutes. Flip the patties once during cooking.)

To make the hummus, place all the hummus ingredients into a food processor or blender, and puree until smooth. Add more garlic, salt, lemon juice, or tahini to taste.

Serve falafel patties in whole wheat pita bread, garnished with hummus, lettuce, tomato, and onion. Alternatively, you can serve the falafel on a bed of lettuce, with hummus on top.

| Each serving contains ½ serving of vegetables, 1 serving of protein, and 2 servings of grain. | |
| --- | --- |
| Protein: 13.5 grams | 19% of calories |
| Fat: 12 grams | 38% of calories |
| Carbs: 31 grams | 44% of calories |
| Calories: 112 | Fiber: 8 grams |

# BLT

Serves 1

*The bacon, lettuce, and tomato sandwich is an American classic. This one uses Yves Canadian veggie bacon, but you can use any other soy bacon that you like. The bread I use is a soy sprouted crunch.*
*This is very close to Zone proportions.*

3 slices veggie bacon
¼ teaspoon olive oil
2 teaspoons soy mayonnaise
2 slices whole grain bread
1 leaf red or green lettuce
2 thick slices tomato

Fry the veggie bacon in a saucepan with a small amount of oil until browned and crispy.

Spread the soy mayonnaise on both slices of the bread, and add the bacon, lettuce, and tomato. Eat up!

Nutritional analysis uses Nayonaise brand soy mayonnaise.
Each serving contains ½ serving of vegetables,
1 to 2 servings of protein, and 2 servings of grain.

| | |
|---|---|
| Protein: 25 grams | 37% of calories |
| Fat: 6 grams | 22% of calories |
| Carbs: 28 grams | 41% of calories |
| Calories: 286 | Fiber: 5 grams |

# Peanut Butter and Apple Sandwich

Serves 1

*This is a real comfort food sandwich. Look for a chunky peanut butter with no added sugar, and remember to use whole grain, high-protein bread, which will bring your net carbs down to about 32.*

2 slices of whole grain bread

2 tablespoons chunky peanut butter

½ apple, sliced thinly

Spread the peanut butter on both slices of the bread. Place the apple slices between them.

Each serving contains 1 serving of fruit, 1 serving of protein, and 2 servings of grain.

| | |
|---|---|
| Protein: 16 grams | 18% of calories |
| Fat: 16 grams | 40% of calories |
| Carbs: 39 grams | 43% of calories |
| Calories: 364 | Fiber: 7.5 grams |

# Cucumber, Mayo, and Avocado Sandwich

Serves 1

*This is a very rich and somewhat indulgent sandwich, high in fat and calories thanks to the avocado. Not to be eaten every day! However, the sandwich is very rich in fiber due to the whole grain bread and the avocado, and the less oil you eat in your diet, the more you can afford to eat nutritious fats like avocadoes and nuts.*

2 teaspoons soy mayonnaise

2 slices whole grain bread

10 slices cucumber (about ⅔ cup)

½ avocado, sliced

Spread the soy mayonnaise on both slices of the bread, and add the cucumber and avocado slices. Eat up!

Nutritional analysis uses Nayonaise brand soy mayonnaise.
Each serving contains 1 serving of vegetables, ½ serving of protein, and 2 servings of grain.

| | |
|---|---|
| Protein: 12.5 grams | 10% of calories |
| Fat: 32 grams | 58% of calories |
| Carbs: 41 grams | 32% of calories |
| Calories: 466 | Fiber: 16 grams |

# Main Dishes

If you're like me, you're thinking about dinner even while you're eating breakfast. I look forward to dinner like very little else in my life, so being able to make food that I love, but that keeps me healthy and keeps my weight in check, is critical.

Yet if you're like me, you're also lazy—for years my husband and I had take-out food delivered for dinner at least three nights a week. While nothing was more exciting than opening the door most evenings and seeing the delivery person with our Chinese or Indian take-out, it was an expensive and fattening habit.

Once I discovered low-carb diets and began working to get my weight under control, it was clear that I would have to do a better job of planning and prepare more meals at home. The result was positive on all fronts. I lost a lot of weight, and my husband and I started to actually enjoy cooking. Plus, I found out planning and cooking meals is fun, and knowing what I'll be cooking all week means I have dinners all week to look forward to.

Because I don't really want to spend hours in the kitchen, most of my recipes are simple to make and don't include that much preparation in advance. I use vegetable bouillon cubes and canned whole beans rather than making my own stock or cooking my own beans. I just can't seem to put the time into these steps. I also use fresh vegetables in every case but one: spinach. After one too many spinach dishes full of sand and grit, I decided that it was just easier to use frozen. (If you love your salad spinner, by all means use fresh spinach as long as you clean it well!)

Feel free to modify these recipes to suit your taste, but keep in mind these basic principles: provide adequate protein, keep the fat content relatively low, use plenty of vegetables, and choose whole grains or those made with soy flour.

# Singapore Stew

Serves 2

*This started out as a turkey dish that I found in a magazine, and it is now one of my favorite entrees. As with many south Asian dishes, the combination of coconut milk with spices and cilantro is exotically delicious. Chinese five-spice powder is found in the spice section or on Asian food shelves in most grocery stores.*

8 ounces (½ pound) seitan, shredded
½ teaspoon Chinese five-spice powder
½ teaspoon hot chili flakes
½ teaspoon salt
Half a 14-ounce can lite coconut milk
½ tablespoon olive oil
2 cloves garlic, peeled, and minced or crushed
1 tablespoon grated peeled fresh ginger
1 cup vegetable stock
1 head bok choy, rinsed, trimmed, and cut into 1-inch pieces
Half a 13-ounce can straw mushrooms
1 plum tomato, chopped
¼ cup sliced scallions
1 tablespoon lime juice
2 tablespoons fresh cilantro leaves

Either the night before or earlier in the day, mix the shredded seitan, Chinese five-spice powder, chili flakes, salt, and coconut milk together in a shallow bowl or pan. Let this mixture marinate for at least two hours.

Pour the oil into a wok over medium-high heat, and add the marinated seitan, keeping the liquid aside. Cook the seitan until browned. Transfer to a plate or bowl.

Add the garlic and ginger to the wok, and stir-fry for about 30 seconds. Slowly add the vegetable stock, seitan, and reserved marinade liquid back into the wok. Simmer for 5 minutes.

Stir in the bok choy, mushrooms, tomato, scallions, and lime juice, and cook, stirring often, until the bok choy leaves are wilted and the stems are barely tender, about 5 more minutes.

Sprinkle with the cilantro and serve.

| Each serving contains 2 servings of vegetable and 2 servings of protein. | |
| --- | --- |
| Protein: 34 grams | 48% of calories |
| Fat: 11 grams | 37% of calories |
| Carbs: 10 grams | 15% of calories |
| Calories: 268 | Fiber: 4 grams |

# Shish Kabob with South Asian Marinade

Serves 2

*This is a great summertime barbecue dish, but you can make it in other seasons indoor as well, using the broiler. The seitan should be marinated in advance, but if you are pressed for time, you can delete that step and just brush the marinade onto the skewers before cooking.*

*Marinade:*

1 tablespoon sesame oil

2 garlic cloves, crushed

2 teaspoons grated peeled fresh ginger

1 red chili, seeded and chopped

1 cup vegetable stock

3 tablespoons soy sauce

¼ teaspoon coriander powder

¼ teaspoon cinnamon

¼ teaspoon nutmeg

¼ teaspoon ground cloves

Salt and pepper to taste

*Shish Kabob:*

4 ounces (¼ pound) seitan, cut into 1-inch chunks

½ zucchini, sliced into 1-inch rounds

½ bell pepper (red, green or yellow, or a mix), sliced into 2-inch squares

½ onion, sliced into wedges

8 mushrooms, cut in half

6 wooden skewers, soaked in cold water for ½ hour

To prepare the marinade, heat the oil in a small saucepan and add the garlic, ginger, and chili. Sauté for 4 to 5 minutes. Add the vegetable stock, soy sauce, and spices, and simmer for about 10 minutes. Cool, then transfer the marinade to a blender or food processor and puree until smooth.

Place the seitan pieces in a shallow bowl or pan, and pour the marinade over them. Let the seitan marinate for at least an hour before you are ready to cook.

Thread the zucchini, bell pepper, onion, mushrooms, and marinated seitan pieces onto the wooden skewers. (Soaking the skewers in water ahead of time will help keep them from charring on the grill.) Brush the skewers with the remaining marinade, and grill or broil, turning several times, until browned and crisp.

| Each serving contains 1 to 2 servings of vegetables and 1 to 2 servings of protein. | |
| --- | --- |
| Protein: 23 grams | 46% of calories |
| Fat: 7.6 grams | 34% of calories |
| Carbs: 10 grams | 20% of calories |
| Calories: 184 | Fiber: 2 grams |

# Saag Tofu with Cauliflower Couscous

*Saag paneer has always been my favorite Indian dish, but if you want to eliminate cheese from your diet, your only other choice in most Indian restaurants is aloo saag, which substitutes high-carb potato for cheese. This recipe combines a wonderful saag base with fried tofu "paneer."*

## Saag:

Two 10-ounce packages frozen
    spinach, or 3 bunches fresh
    spinach, washed, cooked and
    torn into pieces

1 small onion, chopped

2 garlic cloves, crushed

½ teaspoon grated peeled
    fresh ginger

2 tablespoons olive oil

¾ cup plain soy yogurt

½ teaspoon curry powder

½ teaspoon garam masala

Plain soymilk (optional)

## Tofu Paneer:

8 ounces (½ pound) firm tofu,
    drained and cubed

## Couscous:

¾ head chopped cauliflower
    (about 2 cups crumbled)

¼ cup vegetable stock

If you are using fresh spinach, cook it in a covered saucepan with a small amount of water over low heat until the spinach is very soft, about 5 minutes. Transfer to a bowl, drain away the liquid, and let cool. Otherwise, thaw and drain the frozen spinach.

Sauté the onion, garlic, and ginger in half the oil until the onion is translucent and the spices are fragrant.

Puree the cooled, drained spinach and yogurt in a food processor or blender until smooth. If you like your saag creamier, you can also add a bit of plain soymilk while you process.

Add the curry and garam masala powder to the onion mix in the pan, and stir in the spinach and yogurt mix. Stir this mixture and cook for 5 minutes, or until any remaining liquid evaporates.

To prepare the tofu paneer, fry the tofu cubes in the remaining oil until golden brown on all sides. Add the fried tofu paneer to the spinach mix, and cook for 5 minutes more, stirring once or twice.

Chop the cauliflower in a food processor or blender until it is in small pieces about the size of couscous. Pour the vegetable stock into a saucepan, and steam the chopped cauliflower on high heat for no more than 5 minutes. (Use this recipe for other soupy dishes that would taste good served over couscous or rice. You can also sauté the cauliflower in olive oil or steam it.)

Serve saag tofu over cauliflower.

| Each serving contains 3 servings of vegetables and 1 to 2 servings of protein. | |
| --- | --- |
| Protein: 26 grams | 27% of calories |
| Fat: 13 grams | 31% of calories |
| Carbs: 40 grams | 41% of calories |
| Calories: 320 | Fiber: 16 grams |

# Fajitas

## Serves 2

*We make fajitas almost every week in our house. While there are several varieties of low-carb tortillas on the market today, I'm not crazy about the taste or texture of them, so we just eat ours in a bowl topped with salsa and avocado. If you can find a low-carb tortilla that you like, isn't too high in fat, and has a good amount of fiber, feel free to serve your fajitas in those.*

*Marinade:*

¼ cup lime juice

¼ teaspoon cumin

¼ teaspoon cayenne

¼ teaspoon chili powder

I garlic clove

Salt and pepper to taste


6 ounces (⅜ pound) seitan


I tablespoon olive oil

½ medium yellow onion, sliced into large chunks

I cup bell pepper, sliced into I-inch squares

½ zucchini, sliced into ½-inch rounds

2 cups sliced mushrooms

3 scallions, green parts only, sliced into I-inch pieces

To make the marinade, mix the lime juice with the spices in a bowl. Add the seitan pieces and marinate for an hour. Set aside.

In a large nonstick saucepan, heat half the oil over medium heat. Sauté the onions, bell pepper, and zucchini for approximately 5 minutes. Remove vegetables and set aside.

Sauté the mushrooms in the same pan for about 2 minutes, or until the liquid is absorbed. Remove from the heat and set aside.

Pour the remaining oil into the pan, and sauté the seitan for 5 minutes, reserving the marinade. Add all of the vegetables back into the pan, along with the scallion tops and remaining marinade, and cook together for another 1 to 2 minutes.

Serve in a shallow bowl with fresh salsa page 74.

| Each serving contains 3 servings of vegetables and 2 servings of protein. | |
| --- | --- |
| Protein: 26 grams | 45% of calories |
| Fat: 8 grams | 30% of calories |
| Carbs: 14 grams | 24% of calories |
| Calories: 225 | Fiber: 4.3 grams |

# Thai Red Curry Tofu

### Serves 2

*This is one of my favorite Thai foods and is very spicy. You can use the green curry paste for a slightly different flavor if you like (often it's hotter than red curry paste).*

1 teaspoon sesame oil

2 garlic cloves, minced

1 tablespoon minced peeled fresh ginger

2 teaspoons red or green curry paste (or to taste; this is very spicy)

One 14-ounce can lite coconut milk

⅓ cup vegetable stock

½ tablespoon vegetarian oyster sauce

½ tablespoon vegetarian Worcestershire sauce

⅓ cup bamboo shoots

2 cups cauliflower florets

12 ounces (¾ pound) firm tofu, drained and sliced into 1-inch cubes

⅓ cup fresh basil leaves, chopped into strips

Handful of cilantro leaves, chopped

In a medium saucepan, heat the oil and sauté the garlic and ginger for a minute until fragrant. In the same saucepan, simmer the curry paste, coconut milk, vegetable stock, and "oyster" and Worcestershire sauces together for 5 minutes.

Add the bamboo shoots, cauliflower, and tofu. Cover and simmer for at least 15 minutes, or until the cauliflower is tender. Just before serving, add the basil strips and cook for another 2 minutes. Garnish with the cilantro leaves.

Each serving contains 2 servings of vegetables and 1 serving of protein.

| | |
|---|---|
| Protein: 18 grams | 19% of calories |
| Fat: 23 grams | 55% of calories |
| Carbs: 26 grams | 27% of calories |
| Calories: 395 | Fiber: 5 grams |

# Twenty-Minute Chili

### Serves 2

*Chili is the ultimate meal in a bowl, which is probably why it's one of my favorites. It's also easy, tasty, and packed with protein and fiber. This is an excellent meal for the Zone or for South Beach Phase 2. Serve with steamed broccoli or a side salad to increase the vegetable content.*

½ tablespoon olive oil

¼ medium yellow onion, chopped finely

1 cloves garlic, crushed or minced

¼ bell pepper, chopped

½ tablespoon chili powder

½ tablespoon cayenne

½ teaspoon ground cumin

Salt and pepper to taste

1⅓ cups soy hamburger crumbles

Half a 15-ounce can crushed tomatoes

1 cup cooked kidney beans, drained (half a 15-ounce can)

In a large nonstick saucepan, heat the oil over medium heat. Sauté the onions, garlic, and bell pepper for 3 minutes or until the onion turns translucent. Add the chili powder, cayenne, cumin, salt, and pepper. Cook for another 2 minutes.

Add the burger crumbles, tomatoes, and kidney beans. Bring the mixture to a boil. Cover and simmer for another 10 minutes. If you find that the chili is too thick, add ¼ to ½ cup of water.

---

Nutritional analysis uses Morningstar Farms hamburger crumbles.
Each serving contains 2 servings of vegetables and 1 to 2 servings of protein.

| | |
|---|---|
| Protein: 18.5 grams | 28% of calories |
| Fat: 6 grams | 20% of calories |
| Carbs: 34 grams | 52% of calories |
| Calories: 263 | Fiber: 9 grams |

# Tofu in Ginger-Coconut Sauce with Cauliflower Couscous

### Serves 2

*This is one of my all time favorite dishes, and it's also very easy to prepare. Rich with ginger, this delicious recipe is one you'll want to enjoy again and again.*

2 teaspoons peanut oil

3 cloves garlic

1 cup chopped scallions

½ cup finely minced peeled fresh ginger

1 jalapeño pepper, seeded and minced

One 14-ounce can lite coconut milk

2 teaspoons lemon juice

½ cup vegetable stock

12 ounces (¾ pound) firm tofu, drained and cubed

2 cups chopped baby bok choy leaves

1 teaspoon soy sauce

Pepper to taste

1 cup loosely packed chopped cilantro

*Couscous:*

¾ head chopped cauliflower (about 2 cups crumbled)

¼ cup vegetable stock

In a medium saucepan, heat the oil and sauté the garlic, scallions, ginger, and jalapeño for about 30 seconds. Add the coconut milk, lemon juice, and stock, and bring to a boil.

Add the tofu and bok choy to the pot. Simmer, covered, for 10 minutes. Just before serving, add the soy sauce, lots of pepper to taste, and stir in the cilantro leaves.

Chop the cauliflower in a food processor or blender until it's in small pieces about the size of couscous. Pour the vegetable stock into a saucepan and quickly steam the cauliflower pieces for no more than 5 minutes.

Serve the tofu dish over the cauliflower couscous.

| Each serving contains 2 servings of vegetables and 1 to 2 servings of protein. | |
| --- | --- |
| Protein: 19 grams | 23% of calories |
| Fat: 19 grams | 52% of calories |
| Carbs: 20 grams | 24% of calories |
| Calories: 269 | Fiber: 5 grams |

# Tofu Refried Beans

### Serves 2

*This dish is rich with protein and fiber. You can make it with either pinto or*
*black beans. Serve with Taco Salad, pages 74-75.*

1 tablespoon olive oil

½ cup diced onion

3 cloves garlic, minced

2 cups cooked pinto or black beans
  (one 15-ounce can)

1 teaspoon cumin

1 teaspoon cayenne

½ teaspoon chili powder

Salt and pepper to taste

4 ounces (¼ pound) silken tofu

¼ cup diced canned or cooked
  green pepper

In a large saucepan, heat the oil over medium heat. Add the onion and garlic, and sauté until the onion is soft and translucent, about 5 minutes. Stir in the
beans and spices. Mash the beans into the onion mixture. Adjust the spices to
taste. Set aside to cool.

Puree the bean and onion mixture with the tofu in a food processor or
blender until smooth. Return the bean mixture back to the pan, and add in the
green pepper. Reheat and serve.

Each serving contains 1 serving of protein.

| | |
|---|---|
| Protein: 12 grams | 19% of calories |
| Fat: 9 grams | 31% of calories |
| Carbs: 31 grams | 50% of calories |
| Calories: 338 | Fiber: 10.5 grams |

# Weiners and Beans

*Serves 2*

*I loved pork and beans when I was a little girl, and I've continued to long for it 25 years after going vegetarian. Why I didn't figure out how to make it myself is a mystery, now that I realize how easy it is. This is a very filling meal, packed with protein and fiber, bringing the net carbs of this dish down to 29. Serve with a salad.*

1 cup tomato puree

One 15-ounce can white beans

¼ teaspoon paprika

¼ teaspoon turmeric

¼ teaspoon garlic powder

¼ teaspoon mustard powder

1 packet Splenda (optional)

½ teaspoon vinegar

½ teaspoon vegetarian
    Worcestershire sauce

3 tofu or veggie hot dogs, sliced

In a medium saucepan, mix all the ingredients, except for the hot dogs. Bring to a boil and let simmer, uncovered, for 10 minutes to allow the flavors to mingle.

Stir in the tofu dog slices, and heat for another 5 minutes.

Nutritional analysis uses Yves Veggie Dogs.
Each serving contains 1 serving of vegetables and 2 servings of protein.

| | |
|---|---|
| Protein: 30 grams | 40% of calories |
| Fat: 1 gram | 3% of calories |
| Carbs: 43 grams | 57% of calories |
| Calories: 270 | Fiber: 14 grams |

# Soy Sausage Spaghetti

Serves 2

*This pasta dish is super easy to prepare, very filling, has the right combination of carbohydrates, protein, and fat for the Zone, and even has a good fiber content. If you can't find Italian sausage, you can substitute commercially made soy meatballs in this dish.*

2 teaspoons olive oil

½ cup minced onion

2 garlic cloves, minced

½ teaspoon dried Italian spice mix
   (oregano, basil, rosemary, and
   thyme)

1 cup tomato puree

Salt and pepper to taste

1 soy Italian sausage, sliced into
   ¼-inch rounds

4 ounces low-carb pasta

Heat half of the oil in a medium saucepan. Sauté the onions and garlic until the onions are translucent. Add the spices and tomato puree to the onions, and bring to a boil. Simmer the sauce for 15 minutes. Heat the remaining oil in a small saucepan, and brown the sausage rounds.

Bring water to a boil in a 2-quart pot, adding a dash of olive oil to help keep the pasta from clumping together. Cook the pasta according to package instructions; drain. Serve the pasta in shallow bowls with sauce and sausages on top.

Nutritional analysis based on Tofurky brand Italian "sausage" and Soy Deli Soy spaghetti. Each serving contains 1 serving of vegetables, 2 servings of protein, and 1 serving of grain.

| | |
|---|---|
| Protein: 26.5 grams | 29% of calories |
| Fat: 12 grams | 30% of calories |
| Carbs: 36.5 grams | 40% of calories |
| Calories: 362 | Fiber: 4 grams |

# Pasta Puttanesca

Serves 2

*This is my version of the classic pasta puttanesca or "whore's pasta." It supposedly originated in Italian brothels where the ladies could only buy their ingredients once a week, forcing a reliance on basic ingredients. In my house, we make this dish two ways, depending on whether we want a hot dish or a cold one. Both are equally fast and easy. Serve with a salad.*

1 tablespoon olive oil

2 large garlic cloves, minced

6 plum tomatoes, chopped

2 tablespoon capers

6 large basil leaves, sliced into narrow strips

2 tablespoons black olives, sliced

¼ teaspoon red chili pepper flakes

Salt and pepper to taste

4 ounces low-carb soy pasta, cooked according to package directions

*Version 1*: In a mixing bowl, combine the olive oil, garlic, tomatoes, capers, and basil. Serve this "sauce" at room temperature over cooked soy pasta.

*Version 2*: In a medium saucepan, heat the olive oil and sauté the garlic for 1 minute. Add the tomatoes, olives, chili pepper flakes, and salt and pepper. Cook for another 3 to 5 minutes. Remove the sauce from the heat, and stir in the basil. Serve the sauce over the cooked soy pasta.

Each serving contains 1 serving of vegetables, 1 serving of protein, and 1 serving of grain.

| | |
|---|---|
| Protein: 16 grams | 25% of calories |
| Fat: 10 grams | 35% of calories |
| Carbs: 26 grams | 40% of calories |
| Calories: 248 | Fiber: 2 grams |

# Riceless Sushi

Makes 2 rolls

*This is a wonderful way to have sushi without using rice.*
*It tastes just as delicious as traditional vegetarian sushi too! It is somewhat*
*labor intensive, so it makes a great weekend meal.*
*Serve with miso soup and Thai cucumber salad, page 76.*

Have ready:

¼ cucumber, peeled, seeded, and sliced into very thin strips

1 tablespoon rice vinegar

1½ teaspoons sesame oil

2 ounces (⅛ pound) firm tofu, sliced into ½-inch wide, ⅛-inch thick strips, any length

1 cup sliced fresh shiitake mushrooms

Salt and pepper to taste

2 sheets nori (seaweed sheets)

Sushi mat (bamboo mat used to roll sushi rolls)

6 ounces (⅜ pound) well-drained medium-firm tofu, sliced with a cheese slicer into wide but thin strips

½ avocado, sliced

Four 4-inch spears asparagus, steamed until tender

1 scallion, green parts only

Marinate the cucumber strips in the rice vinegar in a shallow bowl. Use ½ teaspoon of the sesame oil to fry the firm tofu strips until browned. Set aside.

Use 1 teaspoon of the oil to sauté the shiitake mushrooms. Add salt and pepper to taste. Set aside.

Once all the fillings are ready, lay out a piece of nori on a sushi mat. Lay half the medium-firm tofu slices on the seaweed, using about half of the seaweed surface. This tofu will serve as the replacement for rice in your sushi rolls. It's critical that you drain this tofu well, or it will make the nori somewhat soggy!

Place half of the mushrooms, avocado, cucumbers, asparagus, scallions, and fried tofu strips lengthwise down the center of the sliced tofu. The fillings should be arranged parallel to the slats of the sushi mat.

To roll, pick up the edge of the seaweed closest to you, with the fillings on it. (The slats of the sushi mat should be running from left to right in front of you.) Start to roll the sushi away from you until you have created a long roll, pressing down slightly to help the roll keep its shape.

When you have rolled it to within about ¾ inch from the far edge of the nori sheet, moisten this edge with a bit of water, then complete your roll to seal. Slice into 1-inch thick pieces. (Slicing on the diagonal makes for interesting shapes.) Repeat with the remaining ingredients. Serve with wasabe paste (Japanese horseradish), thin slices of pickled ginger, and a small bowl of soy sauce for dipping.

---

Each serving contains 1 serving of vegetables and ½ serving of protein.

| | |
|---|---|
| Protein: 8 grams | 22% of calories |
| Fat: 15 grams | 56% of calories |
| Carbs: 13 grams | 22% of calories |
| Calories: 210 | Fiber: 3 grams |

# Spicy Eggplant and Spinach Curry

Serves 2

*If you like curries, this is a great dish for you. It is very high in fiber and low in carbs. Garam masala is a curry spice mixture found in Indian stores, as well as on the spice aisle or Asian foods section of well-stocked supermarkets.*

2 tablespoons canola oil

½ cup chopped yellow onion

2 large garlic cloves, minced

1 tablespoon curry powder

1 teaspoon cayenne

1 tablespoon minced peeled fresh ginger

1 teaspoon jalapeño pepper, seeded and minced

½ eggplant, chopped into 1-inch cubes

½ teaspoon salt

8 ounces frozen spinach, thawed and drained

2 large tomatoes, chopped

½ cup tomato puree

2 teaspoons garam masala

Heat the oil in a large saucepan over medium-high heat. Add the onions, garlic, curry powder and cayenne, and cook for 1 minute. Add the ginger and jalapeño, and cook for another minute.

Add the eggplant and salt, and cook for about 5 minutes, until the eggplant softens.

Add the spinach, tomatoes, and tomato puree, and bring the mixture to a boil. Cover and cook at a simmer for about 15 minutes until it is well blended and the eggplant is very soft. Add the garam masala and cook for another 5 minutes.

Serve as is or over cauliflower couscous (see pages 102-103). To increase the protein content of this dish, you might want to add some fried tofu cubes, as for Saag Tofu, page 102-103

---

Each serving contains 2 servings of vegetables and ½ serving of protein.

| | |
|---|---|
| Protein: 6.5 grams | 11% of calories |
| Fat: 14 grams | 52% of calories |
| Carbs: 23 grams | 38% of calories |
| Calories: 222 | Fiber: 7 grams |

# Spicy Eggplant and Tofu Stir Fry

Serves 2

*This spicy dish is really good, but be sure to use either Japanese or Chinese eggplant, the long, slender, light purple variety (as opposed to the fat, dark purple eggplant most Americans are familiar with).*

1 Japanese eggplant

2 tablespoons sesame oil

1 tablespoon minced peeled fresh ginger

1 tablespoon minced fresh garlic

1 cup burger crumbles

¼ cup soy sauce

1 packet Splenda (optional)

1 tablespoon rice vinegar

1½ teaspoons Asian chili garlic paste

1 teaspoon cornstarch

¼ to 1 cup water

8 ounces (½ pound) extra-firm tofu, drained and cut into 1-inch cubes

¼ cup thinly sliced scallions

Cut the eggplant lengthwise into long quarters, then slice the quarters into ½-inch slices.

Pour 1 tablespoon of the oil into a wok over medium-high heat. Add the eggplant and stir fry until it is soft and lightly browned, about 10 minutes. Remove from the wok and set aside.

Add the ginger and garlic to the wok along with the remaining oil, and sauté, stirring frequently, until fragrant, about 1 minute. Add the burger crumbles and stir for another 3 minutes.

Combine the soy sauce, Splenda (if using), vinegar, chili paste, cornstarch, and ¼ cup water in a small bowl until the cornstarch is blended. Pour the liquid into the wok, and stir until the mixture is simmering and thickened, about 1 minute.

Gently stir in the tofu cubes, cooked eggplant, and scallions, and simmer until the vegetables and tofu are heated through. If the sauce is too thick to adequately cover all the tofu, add more water and continue heating until the flavors are well blended.

---

Nutritional analysis uses Morningstar Farms burger crumbles.
Each serving contains 2 servings of vegetables and 1 serving of protein.

| Protein: 18 grams | 24% of calories |
| Fat: 20 grams | 60% of calories |
| Carbs: 12 grams | 16% of calories |
| Calories: 296 | Fiber: 3 grams |

# Kung Pao Tofu

Serves 2

*The way I prepare it, this dish has no real sauce to speak of except for the very flavorful peanut/chili mixture. However, if you prefer a saucier dish, add a cup of vegetable stock mixed with just enough cornstarch/water mixture to thicken, just before finishing the dish. This is also a high-fat dish, so it should only be for special occasions! Serve with Thai cucumber salad, page 76.*

*Sauce:*

1 tablespoon Asian chili garlic paste

1 packet Splenda (optional)

1 tablespoon sliced scallions

1 teaspoon minced peeled fresh ginger

2 cloves garlic, minced

2 teaspoons sake or sweet white cooking wine

*Tofu:*

1 cup oil

12 ounces (¾ pound) firm tofu, drained and cut into ½-inch cubes

½ cup chopped roasted peanuts

1 tablespoon whole dried red chili peppers, cut in half

1 tablespoon sliced scallions

3 tablespoons water

Up to 1 cup vegetable stock,

    mixed with 1 teaspoon cornstarch (optional)

To make the kung pao sauce, stir together all the ingredients for the sauce in a small bowl. Set aside.

Heat the oil in a wok until it is very hot, and quickly deep fry the tofu cubes in two batches. Set aside on paper towels to drain.

Pour off the oil into a glass or metal container, leaving just enough to coat the wok. On very high heat, add the kung pao sauce, then stir in the peanuts, chili peppers, and scallions. Add the tofu and water, and stir quickly. If you want more sauce, add in 1 cup of cool vegetable stock mixed with 1 teaspoon cornstarch, and stir to coat the tofu and peanuts. Serve immediately.

| Each serving contains 2 servings of protein. | |
| --- | --- |
| Protein: 25 grams | 25% of calories |
| Fat: 29 grams | 65% of calories |
| Carbs: 10 grams | 10% of calories |
| Calories: 413 | Fiber: 3 grams |

# Asparagus and Seitan Stir Fry

Serves 2

*This dish is really flavorful, and the seitan is a terrific source of protein.*

*Marinade:*

2 tablespoons Japanese sake or sweet white cooking wine

2 tablespoons peanut oil

2 tablespoons soy sauce

2 tablespoons rice vinegar

2 large cloves garlic, minced

1 tablespoon minced peeled fresh ginger


5 ounces (about ¼ pound) seitan, shredded and drained

2 cups asparagus, tough ends removed, cut into 2-inch pieces
 (about 1 pound)

2 cups sliced mushrooms

½ cup snow peas, ends trimmed


Mix the marinade ingredients together in a medium bowl. Add the seitan pieces to the marinade, and set aside for at least an hour (refrigerate if longer) until ready to use.

Heat a wok, and add the seitan pieces, along with enough of the marinade to lightly cover, reserving the remainder of the liquid. Cook the seitan over very high heat until the seitan is heated through and slightly browned. Remove from the wok and set aside.

Add the asparagus and mushrooms to the wok along with the reserved marinade, and steam for 3 minutes on high heat.

Add ¼ to ½ cup water and cover the wok, letting the mixture simmer for approximately 5 minutes, until the asparagus is tender. (The exact time will depend on the thickness of the asparagus).

When the asparagus is ready, return the seitan to the wok along with the snow peas, and stir until the flavors are well blended and the snow peas are just hot.

Each serving contains 4 servings of vegetables and 2 servings of protein.

| | |
|---|---|
| Protein: 27.5 grams | 41% of calories |
| Fat: 8 grams | 26% of calories |
| Carbs: 22 grams | 33% of calories |
| Calories: 263 | Fiber: 6 grams |

# Three-Mushroom Tofu Stir Fry

Serves 2

*You can make this with any combination of mushrooms. I used oyster, shiitake, and button mushrooms, but you can try wood ear and straw mushrooms as well.*

1 tablespoon sesame oil

2 tablespoons minced peeled fresh ginger

2 large cloves garlic, minced

¼ teaspoon Chinese five-spice powder

3 cups sliced mushrooms

8 ounces (½ pound) extra-firm tofu, drained and sliced into ½ - x 1-inch pieces

1 cup packed baby bok choy leaves

1 tablespoon soy sauce

½ cup chopped scallions

1 teaspoon cornstarch

1 cup vegetable stock

In a wok, heat the oil and stir fry the ginger, garlic, and Chinese five-spice powder for about 1 minute, until fragrant. Add the mushrooms and sauté for another 3 minutes. Add the tofu and sauté with the mushrooms for another 5 minutes. Add the bok choy, soy sauce, and scallions, and cook for another 2 minutes.

Add the cornstarch mixed with the vegetable stock to the wok and simmer, stirring constantly, until the sauce is well thickened.

Each serving contains 3 servings of vegetables and 1 serving of protein.

| | |
|---|---|
| Protein: 12 grams | 28% of calories |
| Fat: 12 grams | 60% of calories |
| Carbs: 6 grams | 13% of calories |
| Calories: 203 | Fiber: 1.5 grams |

# Summer Stew

Serves 2

*My sister sent me this very easy recipe that was originally made with couscous. I've modified it by substituting cauliflower for couscous.*

2 cups cauliflower florets

1 tablespoon olive oil

½ medium yellow onion, coarsely chopped

1 large garlic clove, minced

1 zucchini, sliced

1 crookneck squash, sliced

¾ cup vegetable stock

2 plum tomatoes

1 cup cooked white beans

½ cup coarsely chopped fresh basil leaves

Salt and pepper to taste

Process the cauliflower florets in a food processor or blender until they are the consistency of couscous. You should have enough to give you 1 cup.

In a medium saucepan, heat the oil and sauté the onions and garlic until the onions are translucent. Add the zucchini and crookneck squash to the saucepan, stirring constantly. Add the cauliflower "couscous" and vegetable stock. Stir for about 5 minutes.

Add the tomatoes, beans, basil, salt, and pepper. Cook, uncovered, for 5 to 10 minutes, stirring from time to time, until the squash is tender and much of the broth has evaporated.

Each serving contains 3 servings of vegetables and ½ serving of protein.

| | |
|---|---|
| Protein: 7.5 grams | 13% of calories |
| Fat: 7.4 grams | 29% of calories |
| Carbs: 33 grams | 58% of calories |
| Calories: 200 | Fiber: 10.5 grams |

# Tofu Yung

Serves 2

*This is a soy-based version of the classic egg fu yung. It's quite tasty! This is the only recipe in this book that calls for blending firm tofu (rather than silken) in a food processor.*

*Patties:*

1 cup snow peas, ends trimmed, cut into 1-inch pieces

½ cup sliced button mushrooms

4 scallions, cut into 1-inch pieces

½ cup bamboo shoots, sliced into halves

1 tablespoon sesame oil

1 cup fresh bean sprouts

14 ounces (⅞ pound) firm tofu

1 tablespoon soy sauce

⅓ cup soy flour

1 teaspoon baking powder

*Gravy:*

1 cup diced button mushrooms

1 teaspoon sesame oil

2 tablespoons soy sauce

1 cup cool vegetable stock

1 tablespoon cornstarch

In a large wok over medium-high heat, stir fry the snow peas, mushrooms, scallions, and bamboo shoots in the sesame oil until the vegetables are tender, about 5 minutes. Add in the bean sprouts, remove from the heat, and set aside.

Blend the tofu and soy sauce in a food processor or blender until very smooth and creamy. Transfer to a bowl and mix in the soy flour and baking powder. Mix in the stir fried vegetables.

Preheat the oven to 325°F. Form four patties out of the mixture (which will be very soft), and place on a nonstick or well-oiled baking sheet. Bake for 30 minutes. Flip the patties and bake for another 15 minutes.

Using the same wok as you used for the vegetables, make the gravy by sautéing the mushrooms in the sesame oil for about 3 minutes. Mix the soy sauce, vegetable stock, and cornstarch, pour over the mushrooms, and cook over low heat until thickened.

Serve the patties hot from the oven with the gravy poured on top.

| Each serving contains 3 servings of vegetables and 1 serving of protein. | |
| --- | --- |
| Protein: 18.5 grams | 21% of calories |
| Fat: 15 grams | 38% of calories |
| Carbs: 38 grams | 42% of calories |
| Calories: 333 | Fiber: 3.5 grams |

# Cauliflower "Potatoes"

Serves 2

*Almost every low-carb cookbook has a recipe for baked or mashed potatoes using cauliflower, and here are mine. These are not main dishes but tasty and rich side dishes. Version 1 is similar to mashed potatoes and can be served with mushroom gravy on top. Version 2 is more like baked potatoes and should be served with chopped scallions or chives. Accompany these with any protein-rich dish.*

*Version 1:*
½ head cauliflower (about 2 cups)
2 tablespoons plain soymilk
2 tablespoons nonhydrogenated margarine
Salt and pepper to taste

Steam the cauliflower until it's very soft. Drain the cooking water and mash the cauliflower with the soymilk, margarine, and spices. Top with the gravy of your choice or eat as is.

*Version 2:*

½ head cauliflower (about 2 cups)

2 tablespoons nonhydrogenated margarine

¼ cup soy sour cream

¼ teaspoon paprika

¼ teaspoon cayenne

Salt and pepper to taste

¼ cup chopped scallions or chives

Steam the cauliflower until it's very soft. Drain the cooking water and mash the cauliflower with the margarine, sour cream, and spices. Top with scallions or chives.

Nutritional analysis uses Tofutti Sour Supreme soy sour cream.
Each serving contains 2 servings of vegetables.

| | |
|---|---|
| Protein: 3 grams | 7% of calories |
| Fat: 16 grams | 78% of calories |
| Carbs: 7 grams | 15% of calories |
| Calories: 178 | Fiber: 4 grams |

# Beefy Mushroom Stroganoff

### Serves 2

*This is another classic comfort food, updated to be healthy, compassionate, and low-carb. This dish can be served as is, in a bowl, or over a single serving (2 ounces) of the low-carb pasta of your choice.*

1 tablespoon olive oil

⅓ cup chopped onion

1 clove garlic, chopped

2 cups sliced mushrooms

2 tablespoons cooking sherry
(optional)

1 teaspoon paprika

1½ cups vegetarian burger crumbles

1 tablespoon vegetarian
Worcestershire sauce

¼ cup soy sour cream

Salt and pepper to taste

In a heavy saucepan, heat the oil and sauté the onion and garlic until the onion is soft and translucent.

Add the mushrooms and sherry, and continue cooking until the mushrooms are soft. Add the paprika, followed by the burger crumbles and Worcestershire sauce. Remove from the heat, stir in the sour cream, and add salt and pepper to taste.

Nutritional analysis uses Morningstar Farms burger crumbles
and Tofutti Sour Supreme soy sour cream.
Each serving contains 2 servings of vegetables and 1 serving of protein.
With pasta, add 1 serving of grain.

| | |
|---|---|
| Protein: 13 grams | 28% of calories |
| Fat: 11 grams | 51% of calories |
| Carbs: 10 grams | 21% of calories |
| Calories: 166 | Fiber: 4 grams |

# Snacks and Hors d'Oeuvres

Many nutritionists, including proponents of both the South Beach and Zone diets, recommend eating five times per day: three meals plus two snacks.

Why snack? By eating frequently throughout the day, you'll keep your blood sugar levels from dropping too low, ensuring that you won't become so hungry that you'll overeat.

According the Zone, you should never go five waking hours without eating, meaning that you will have a snack between lunch and dinner, and a snack or dessert after dinner.

Like other meals, snacks should be planned so that they are not just satisfying, but are healthful and fit within the parameters of the low-carb diet. (They should also be planned to keep you from running to the vending machine!) Make sure that your snacks include protein and vegetable- or grain-based carbohydrates, so that they'll fill you up and keep your blood sugar levels even (especially if you're on South Beach or the Zone).

You can use some of the soups, salads, or main dishes from the other chapters as snacks, as long as the serving size is about one-fourth or one-third the amount that you would consume in a meal.

Besides being good for snacking, there are some recipes in this chapter that would also make wonderful hors d'oeuvres for parties.

# Mock Lunchmeat Rollups

## Serves 1

*If you're like me, even if you had breakfast and lunch, you may still get hungry at around 3 or 4 PM in the afternoon. We don't eat dinner at my house till late, and I can't wait another four hours to eat (nor should you). This is a super quick, easy-to-make snack that is very low in carbohydrates, low in fat, and gives you that extra push you need to get through the rest of your afternoon.*

½ teaspoon soy mayonnaise

3 slices vegetarian cold cuts (turkey, salami, or bologna)

3 red bell pepper strips (other good choices are green or yellow bell pepper or celery)

1 scallion, sliced into thirds

Place a dab of soy mayonnaise on each slice of lunchmeat, add a slice of bell pepper and a piece of scallion, and roll up.

---

Nutritional analysis uses Yves Veggie turkey and Nayonaise soy mayonnaise.
Each serving contains ½ serving of vegetables and 1 serving of protein.

---

| | |
|---|---|
| Protein: 13 grams | 64% of calories |
| Fat: 0.5 grams | 6% of calories |
| Carbs: 6 grams | 30% of calories |
| Calories: 80 | Fiber: 2 grams |

# Deviled Tofu with Celery

Serves 1

*What a yummy snack! The deviled tofu can be made in a larger quantity and used for sandwiches on whole grain bread or whole wheat pita bread.*

2 ounces (⅛ pound) soft tofu, crumbled
½ scallion, chopped
1 teaspoon soy mayonnaise
½ teaspoon Dijon mustard
¼ teaspoon capers
½ teaspoon sweet relish
⅛ teaspoon curry powder
Salt and pepper to taste
2 celery stalks

In a mixing bowl, combine the tofu, scallion, soy mayonnaise, mustard, capers, relish, and spices.

Spoon the deviled tofu into the celery stalks.

Nutritional analysis uses Nayonaise brand soy mayonnaise.
Each serving contains 1 serving of vegetables.

| | |
|---|---|
| Protein: 4.7 grams | 29% of calories |
| Fat: 3 grams | 47% of calories |
| Carbs: 4 grams | 24% of calories |
| Calories: 74 | Fiber: 2 grams |

# Quickie Snacks

*There are times when you just need a snack and taking the time to follow a recipe just won't do. Here are some low-carb snacks to grab when you really need a quick bite.*

*Edamame*, or whole soybeans, are an excellent snack. Buy them fresh or frozen, and shell and eat them at room temperature with a little salt. Eat about ½ cup of shelled soybeans per snack: 8 grams protein, 3 grams fat, 9 grams carbs, 4 grams fiber, 100 calories

*Nuts* are a good, albeit high-fat, snack. They are high in protein and low in carbs. Eat no more than about 20 nuts (or 1 ounce) for a snack: 5 grams protein, 16 grams fat, 6 grams carbs, 2 grams fiber, 170 calories

*Fruit* can be a low-carbohydrate snack, although it has virtually no protein, so it won't do for a Zone snack (but could be combined with nuts or baked tofu). Choose from the lowest carb fruits, such as apples, apricots, blueberries, cantaloupe, cherries, grapefruit, grapes, kiwi, mangoes, oranges, peaches, pears, plums, and strawberries. These will all contain anywhere from 50 to 80 calories, from 2 to 8 grams of fiber, and from 5 to 20 carbs per serving, with little to no protein and no fat at all.

*Popcorn* is really a low-carb snack. When air-popped, it also contains very little fat. A cup of air-popped popcorn only contains 6 carbohydrates and 31 calories.

*Ready-baked tofu* is one of the easiest snacks to eat, and is high in protein and low in carbohydrates. Look in the deli or soy section of your local grocery store for brands such as Wildwood and Soy Deli. My favorites are the smoked flavors, but there are a great many for you to choose from. Most will contain about 14 grams protein, 6 grams fat, 11 grams carbohydrate, 2 grams fiber, and 150 calories for a 3-ounce serving, but a snack would probably be about 2 ounces or ⅛ pound.

# Italian Tofu Stuffed Mushrooms

Makes about 1 cup of filling,
enough for approximately 4 dozen mushrooms.
Serving size equals 8 mushrooms.

*This is a wonderful hors d'oeuvre for a cocktail party. Serving these mushrooms will make your friends think you're a gourmet cook.*

4 dozen medium button
    mushrooms, washed and stems
    removed
4 tablespoons olive oil
4 tablespoons cooking sherry
Salt and pepper to taste

*Filling:*

6 ounces (⅜ pound) silken tofu
8 pitted kalamata olives
2 small garlic cloves
¼ cup basil leaves
¼ cup artichoke hearts

In a large saucepan, sauté the mushrooms in olive oil for 2 minutes. Add the sherry, salt, and pepper to the mushrooms, and continue sautéing until most of the liquid is absorbed and the mushrooms are soft and browned.

Set the mushrooms bottom up on an ungreased baking sheet, reserving any leftover liquid. Process all the ingredients for the filling, along with the leftover mushroom liquid, in a food processor or blender until very smooth.

Preheat the oven to 350°F. Spoon the mixture (about 1 teaspoon per mushroom) into the mushroom caps. Bake for 10 minutes.

| Each serving contains 1 serving of vegetables. | |
| --- | --- |
| Protein: 10 grams | 22% of calories |
| Fat: 11 grams | 57% of calories |
| Carbs: 9 grams | 21% of calories |
| Calories: 141 | Fiber: 0 grams |

# Baked Tofu Triangles

Makes about Z\x cup of filling, enough for approximately 2 dozen triangles.
Serving size equals 6 triangles.

*This is a way to make and eat a yummy olive tapenade, but without the crackers or bread that you would usually serve it on.*

## Tapenade:

½ cup pitted kalamata olives

¼ cup soft sun-dried tomatoes

¼ cup marinated artichoke hearts

2 tablespoons capers

1 teaspoon Dijon mustard

16 ounces (1 pound) firm tofu, drained

Using a chopper or sharp knife, chop all of the tapenade ingredients up finely together. Set aside.

To make the tofu triangles, slice through a narrow side of a block of tofu, making 3 slices about ½-inch thick. Stack the slices and cut through the stack diagonally, making triangles.

Preheat the oven to 350°F. Oil a baking sheet and arrange the tofu triangles on it. Bake for 45 minutes. Remove the triangles from the baking sheet, and place them on a serving plate. Spread 1 teaspoon tapenade on each triangle. Serve immediately.

Each serving contains ⅓ serving of protein.

| | |
|---|---|
| Protein: 4 grams | 14% of calories |
| Fat: 5.5 grams | 46% of calories |
| Carbs: 10 grams | 39% of calories |
| Calories: 111 | Fiber: 2 grams |

# Artichoke Olive Dip with Fennel Crudites

Makes about 1½ cups of dip. Serving size equals about ½ cup.

*This is an unusual-tasting dip, perfect for people who like the rich, fragrant flavor of artichokes. If you're not crazy about the taste of fennel, feel free to use celery instead.*

*Dip:*

2 cups drained marinated whole artichoke hearts

1 tablespoon olive oil

1 large garlic clove, minced

½ cup pitted brine-cured green olives

Salt and pepper to taste

2 tablespoons finely chopped fresh parsley leaves

*Accompaniment:*

2 medium fennel bulbs (sometimes called anise), stalks trimmed flush with bulbs and bulbs cut lengthwise into strips or triangles for dipping

In a food processor or blender, puree the artichoke hearts with the oil, garlic, and olives until very smooth, about 3 minutes. Transfer the puree to a bowl, and stir in the salt and pepper to taste. Cover and chill the dip for at least 4 hours and up to 24 hours. Stir in the chopped parsley just before serving. Serve the dip with the fennel strips.

| Each serving contains 1 serving of vegetables. | |
| --- | --- |
| Protein: 3 grams | 12% of calories |
| Fat: 7.5 grams | 64% of calories |
| Carbs: 6 grams | 24% of calories |
| Calories: 110 | Fiber: 0 grams |

# Roasted Garlic, Onion, and Red Pepper Hummus

Makes about 4 cups of dip. Serving size equals about ½ cup.

*This is a hummus that's made with roasted vegetables, giving it a richer flavor than traditional hummus.*

1 garlic head, halved crosswise

1 medium onion, peeled and halved crosswise

2 tablespoons olive oil

2 red bell peppers

6 ounces (⅜ pound) silken tofu

10 kalamata olives or other brine-cured black olives, pitted

1 tablespoon drained capers

1½ cups garbanzo beans

¼ cup tahini

¼ cup lemon juice

½ teaspoon salt, or more to taste

Preheat the oven to 375°F. Place the garlic and onion halves open side down on a small oiled baking sheet. Brush with the olive oil, and roast about 30 minutes, until the onion is tender and the garlic is golden and tender, turning over halfway through baking. Cool.

Broil the bell peppers on all sides until black, bubbly and crispy. Place hot into a small paper bag; close the bag and set aside so the peppers will steam. In about 20 minutes, remove the peppers and carefully peel off the skins. Slice open the peppers and remove the seeds and core.

Squeeze or scoop the garlic from its skin. Cut each onion half into quarters, removing any hardened skin.

Puree the roasted garlic and onion, blackened and peeled red bell pepper, tofu, olives, capers, garbanzo beans, tahini, and lemon juice in a food processor or blender. Transfer to a serving bowl or container, and add salt to taste. Cover and refrigerate for about 2 hours.

Serve with crudités or high-fiber whole grain crackers.

| Each serving contains 1 serving of vegetables. | |
| --- | --- |
| Protein: 5 grams | 14% of calories |
| Fat: 9 grams | 55% of calories |
| Carbs: 11 grams | 31% of calories |
| Calories: 139 | Fiber: 2.5 grams |

# Spiced Mixed Nuts

Makes 1 cup of nuts. Serving size equals 1 ounce or 2 tablespoons.

*These taste like the Chex party mix of your childhood, but without all the carbs—and you don't have to cook them either. They are pretty high fat, so eat them in moderation!*

1 cup mixed whole, shelled unsalted nuts

¼ teaspoon salt

¼ teaspoon cayenne pepper

¼ teaspoon cumin

¼ teaspoon chili pepper

Place the nuts with the spices in a plastic bag, and shake. Serve!

---

Each serving contains ⅓ serving of protein.

| | |
|---|---|
| Protein: 5 grams | 11% of calories |
| Fat: 16 grams | 77% of calories |
| Carbs: 6 grams | 13% of calories |
| Calories: 170 | Fiber: 2 |

# *Desserts*

If you're used to eating dessert, giving it up when dieting is one of the hardest parts of trying to lose weight.

Yet even if you do eliminate dessert, the time between dinner and bedtime is one of the more dangerous times of the day for forbidden food, especially if, like me, you watch a lot of television. There's something about sitting in front of the TV on an overstuffed couch, surrounded by always-hungry animals, which makes me want to eat mindlessly.

But with a little planning, you can make yummy, satisfying desserts that will satisfy your sweet tooth and your need for a post-dinner snack, yet won't contribute to your thighs.

Dessert can be as simple as a handful of nuts along with some fruit, or it can be as complicated as the chocolate mousse recipe in this chapter. Many of the recipes call for an ice cream maker, but luckily you can do the actual cranking on the couch!

# Strawberry Tofu Sorbet

### Serves 2

*This creamy strawberry dish is an excellent ice cream substitute. You'll need an ice cream maker to make this.*

6 ounces (⅜ pound) silken tofu

1 tablespoon frozen orange juice concentrate

½ teaspoon vanilla

½ cup sliced strawberries, (about 4 medium)

1 pack Splenda or other sugar-free sweetener

In a blender or food processor, combine all of the ingredients and blend until smooth. Pour into a medium mixing bowl.

To quick chill, nest the bowl of sorbet in a larger bowl filled partially with ice water. Stir often until cold, about 5 minutes; otherwise, put the bowl of sorbet into the refrigerator for at least an hour.

Pour the chilled sorbet into an ice cream maker. Freeze according to the machine's directions.

Each serving contains ⅓ serving of protein and ½ serving of fruit.

| | |
|---|---|
| Protein: 5 grams | 23% of calories |
| Fat: 2.5 grams | 26% of calories |
| Carbs: 11 grams | 50% of calories |
| Calories: 85 | Fiber: 1 gram |

# Blackberry Ice

### Serves 2

*This sorbet has a surprisingly high fiber content for such a small dessert.*

6 ounces (⅜ pound) silken tofu

4 ounces frozen blackberries (about 1 cup)

1 tablespoon frozen apple juice concentrate

1 tablespoon soy yogurt

½ teaspoon vanilla

1 packet Splenda or other sugar-free sweetener

In a blender or food processor, combine all of the ingredients and blend until smooth.

To quick chill, nest the bowl of sorbet in a larger bowl filled partially with ice water. Stir often until cold, about 5 minutes; otherwise, put the bowl of sorbet into the refrigerator for at least an hour.

Pour the chilled sorbet into an ice cream maker. Freeze according to the machine's directions.

| Each serving contains ⅓ serving of protein and 1 serving of fruit. | |
| --- | --- |
| Protein: 6 grams | 23% of calories |
| Fat: 2.5 grams | 22% of calories |
| Carbs: 14 grams | 55% of calories |
| Calories: 101 | Fiber: 4 grams |

# Piña Colada Tofu Sorbet

### Serves 2

*I love anything with coconut or pineapple in it, so this dessert is a real treat. Look for cream of coconut (a sweetened product, not the same as coconut milk or cream) in the section of the store where liquor and mixers are sold.*

6 ounces (⅜ pound) silken tofu

1 cup chopped pineapple

1 teaspoon vanilla

2 tablespoons cream of coconut

1 packet Splenda or other sugar-free sweetener

In a blender or food processor, combine all of the ingredients and blend until smooth.

To quick chill, nest the bowl of sorbet in a larger bowl filled partially with ice water. Stir often until cold, about 5 minutes; otherwise, put the bowl of sorbet into the refrigerator for at least an hour.

Pour the chilled sorbet into an ice cream maker. Freeze according to the machine's directions.

| Each serving contains ⅓ serving of protein and 1 serving of fruit. | |
| --- | --- |
| Protein: 5 grams | 14% of calories |
| Fat: 5 grams | 31% of calories |
| Carbs: 21 grams | 56% of calories |
| Calories: 145 | Fiber: 1 gram |

# Chocolate Coconut Mousse

Serves 2

*This dessert reminds me of growing up outside of San Diego and riding on the bus for two hours to get to the beach. The smell of coconut oil (in the days before we knew about skin cancer) was omnipresent, and to this day, coconut still makes me think of the beach.*

6 ounces (⅜ pound) silken tofu

1 tablespoon unsweetened cocoa powder

1 teaspoon vanilla

3 tablespoons cream of coconut *(see comments on facing page)*

1 tablespoon frozen apple juice concentrate

2 packets Splenda or other sugar-free sweetener

In a blender or food processor, combine all of the ingredients and blend until smooth.

Chill for an hour and serve.

| Each serving contains ⅓ serving of protein. | |
| --- | --- |
| Protein: 5 grams | 15% of calories |
| Fat: 5 grams | 34% of calories |
| Carbs: 17 grams | 51% of calories |
| Calories: 131 | Fiber: 1 gram |

# Coconut Strawberry Pudding

### Serves 2

*This is another tasty and easy-to-make ice creamy-dessert, perfect for coconut lovers like myself.*

6 ounces (⅜ pound) silken tofu

½ cup sliced fresh strawberries (about 4 medium)

½ cup shredded unsweetened coconut

½ teaspoon vanilla

1 packet Splenda or other sugar-free sweetener (or more if you like your desserts sweeter)

In a blender or food processor, combine all of the ingredients and blend until smooth.

Chill for an hour and serve.

---

Each serving contains ⅓ serving of protein and ½ serving of fruit.

| | |
|---|---|
| Protein: 5 grams | 26% of calories |
| Fat: 2.5 grams | 29% of calories |
| Carbs: 9 grams | 45% of calories |
| Calories: 77 | Fiber: 1 gram |

# Chocolate-Dipped Strawberries

Serves 2

*This is a very decadent-tasting dessert but isn't actually all that sinful. Look for chocolate that contains no dairy, especially from fair trade companies such as Dagoba, Endangered Species, and Green & Black's. If you can't find Hip Whip for this recipe in your local grocery store (it's usually in the freezer section near the Cool Whip), you can make it yourself with the Tofu Whipping Topping recipe on page 148.*

I ounce semisweet or bittersweet chocolate

I tablespoon Hip Whip

Dash of vanilla extract

4 strawberries

Melt the chocolate and Hip Whip in a microwave-safe bowl or cup in the microwave for 30 seconds, or until very soft. Stir once before completely melted to combine the ingredients, then stir in the vanilla extract and cool slightly.

Dip each strawberry in the melted chocolate, allowing any excess to drip off. Place the strawberries upside down on waxed paper or other nonstick surface, and set in the refrigerator for at least 15 minutes, or until the chocolate has hardened.

---

Each serving contains ½ serving of fruit.

| | |
|---|---|
| Protein: I gram | 6% of calories |
| Fat: 5.3 grams | 52% of calories |
| Carbs: 10 grams | 42% of calories |
| Calories: 99 | Fiber: I gram |

# Tofu Whipped Topping

Serves 4

5 ounces (⅓ cup) drained soft silken tofu, blotted dry with a towel

2 packets Splenda or other sugar-free sweetener

1 tablespoon canola oil

1 teaspoon pure vanilla extract

¼ teaspoon fresh lemon juice

Process the tofu, Splenda, oil, vanilla, and lemon juice in a blender or food processor until smooth and creamy.

Transfer to a small container, cover, and refrigerate for 30 minutes before serving. This topping should be used within a few hours after making it.

| | |
|---|---|
| Protein: 2 grams | 14% of calories |
| Fat: 5 grams | 73% of calories |
| Carbs: 2 grams | 13% of calories |
| Calories: 51 | Fiber: 0 gram |

# Raspberries with Hip Whip

Serves 1

*This isn't so much of a recipe as an idea for a very low-cal simple dessert. The only thing you have to remember is to thaw the Hip Whip before snacking. If you can't find Hip Whip for this recipe in your local grocery store (it's usually in the freezer section near the Cool Whip), you can make it yourself with the Tofu Whipping Topping recipe on the facing page.*

10 raspberries

2 tablespoons Hip Whip*

Thaw the Hip Whip about an hour before you're ready for dessert. Place the raspberries into a bowl. Cover with the Hip Whip and eat!

Each serving contains ¼ serving of fruit.

| | |
|---|---|
| Protein: 0 grams | 0% of calories |
| Fat: 0.75 grams | 27% of calories |
| Carbs: 4.5 grams | 73% of calories |
| Calories: 32 | Fiber: 1 gram |

# Chocolate Mousse

*My parents sent me this recipe, and it's one of my favorites. This is a very rich and indulgent dessert, and is higher in fat, calories, and carbs than a typical snack, so save this for special occasions. As with any other dish made with chocolate chips or baking chocolate, look for brands that do not contain dairy.*

6 ounces (⅜ pound) silken tofu

½ cup high-quality bittersweet or semisweet chocolate, coarsely chopped, or chocolate chips (2½ ounces)

1 tablespoon dark rum or Grand Marnier

1 packet Splenda or other sugar-free sweetener

½ teaspoon vanilla

1 tablespoon sliced almonds, toasted*

In a small saucepan, heat ⅓ of the silken tofu until it just boils, whisking constantly. Watch carefully so that it doesn't scorch. Remove the liquid tofu from the heat, and stir in the coarsely chopped chocolate or chocolate chips. Let stand until melted.

Add the rum or Grand Marnier, and whisk thoroughly to combine the ingredients. The mixture will appear grainy. Let cool slightly.

In a food processor or blender, puree the remaining silken tofu with the Splenda and vanilla until it's smooth and creamy. Add the melted chocolate mixture, and puree until thoroughly blended, smooth, and creamy. (If this doesn't get smooth enough in your food processor, try it in your blender.)

Pour the mousse into dessert dishes and refrigerate until set, at least 2 hours. Garnish each dish with the toasted sliced almonds and serve.

*To toast almonds, heat the oven to 375°F. Place the almonds in an ungreased pie pan, and bake for 2 to 3 minutes until just slightly browned. Watch carefully so they don't scorch.

| Each serving contains ⅓ serving of protein. | |
| --- | --- |
| Protein: 7 grams | 11% of calories |
| Fat: 14 grams | 48% of calories |
| Carbs: 28 grams | 41% of calories |
| Calories: 246 | Fiber: 0 grams |

*Note: There is not a huge difference between semi-sweet and bittersweet chocolate with respect to the nutritional analysis. But some brands are actually different, so you may want shop around if you have a lot of choices. I made this with Guitard semi-sweet chocolate chips.*

# Pineapple Lime Sorbet

Serves 2

*This one is very LIMEY.*

2 cups chopped fresh pineapple
6 ounces (⅜ pound) silken tofu
⅓ cup fresh lime juice

Arrange the pineapple pieces in a single layer on a baking sheet, sheet of wax paper, or piece of aluminum foil, and freeze for at least 1 hour.

Combine the frozen pineapple chunks, tofu and lime juice in a food processor or blender. Process until the mixture is smooth. Serve immediately.

Each serving contains ⅓ serving of protein and 2 servings of fruit.

| | |
|---|---|
| Protein: 5 grams | 13% of calories |
| Fat: 2.5 grams | 14% of calories |
| Carbs: 29 grams | 73% of calories |
| Calories: 158 | Fiber: 2 grams |

# PRODUCT REFERENCES

Depending on where you live, you may not have access to all the brands that I've listed below. But hopefully you can find at least one brand of each type of food.

The following companies make meatless cold cuts, bacon, sausage, burgers, hot dogs, roasts, ribs, jerky, and even vegetarian "seafood":

Boca Foods (Boca Burger)

Garden Burger

Lightlife

Loma Linda

Morningstar Farms

Primal Spirit

Quorn

Soy Deli

Turtle Island

Vegi-Deli

Wildwood

Worthington

Yves

There are also a number of companies that make dried versions of meat alternatives, but I don't recommend that you purchase those without checking the nutritional counts first. Many of these products are higher in carbohydrates. The general rule to go by with a meat substitute is that the protein count should be at least twice as high as the carbohydrate count.

Finally, the most popular brands of soy mayonnaises are:

Vegenaise

Nayonaise

Wildwood makes wonderful flavors of aïoli that I love using. They're a bit higher in fat than these mayonnaises, but make a nice treat.

Online sources to purchase meat substitutes and other vegetarian products:

healthy-eating.com/

veganstore.com

vegetarianstore.com/

vegecyber.com/

## REFERENCES

Agatston, Arthur. *The South Beach Diet.* New York: Rodale Press. 2003.

Atkins, Robert CUP. *Atkins for Life: The Complete Controlled Carb Program for Permanent Weight Loss and Good Health.* New York: St. Martin's Press. 2003.

Associated Press. *"FDA to Decide What's Really a Low-Carb Food."* March 17, 2004.

carbohydrate-counter.org

Fumento, Michael. *"Big Fat Fake: The Atkins Diet Controversy and the Sorry State of Science Journalism."* Reason, March 2003.

Green, Patrice, and Solin, Allison Lee. *"Deadly Dieting: The Truth behind the Atkins Plan."* PCRM website, www.pcrm.org

Low-Carb Living. *"Study Links Glycemic Load to Colorectal Cancer."* March/April 2004, p. 17.

Ness, Carol. *"Curbing Carbs: Dieters Belly Up to the Bar for Atkins Style Libations."* San Francisco Chronicle, March 18, 2004.

Physicians Committee for Responsible Medicine. *"Analysis of Health Problems Associated with High-Protein, High-Fat, Carbohydrate-Restricted Diets Reported via an Online Registry."* November 2003

Sears, Barry. *The Soy Zone.* New York: Regan Books. 2001.

Ward, Elizabeth. *The Low-Carb Bible: Your All-in-One Guide to Successful Low-Carb Dieting.* Lincolnwood, IL: Publications International, Ltd. 2003.

Willet, Walter CUP, and Skerrett, Patrick. *"Going Beyond Atkins."* Newsweek, January 19, 2004, pp. 45-48.

# Index

# BOOK PUBLISHING COMPANY

*since 1974—books that educate, inspire, and empower*

To find your favorite vegetarian and soyfood products online, visit:

## www.healthy-eating.com

The Ultimate Uncheese
Cookbook
Jo Stepaniak
1-57067-151-6  $15.95

The New Becoming Vegetarian
Vesanto Melina, R.D.,
Brenda Davis, R.D.,
1-57067-144-3  $19.95

Stevia
Natural Sweetener for Drinks,
Desserts, Baked Goods & More
Rita DePuydt
1-57067-133-8  $14.95

More Fabulous Beans
Barb Bloomfield
1-57067-146-X  $14.95

The Fiber for Life Cookbook
Bryanna Clark Grogan
1-57067-134-6  $12.95

Purchase these health titles and cookbooks from your local bookstore or
natural food store, or you can buy them directly from:

Book Publishing Company • P.O. Box 99 • Summertown, TN 38483
1-800-695-2241

*Please include $3.95 per book for shipping and handling.*